Chef Tell's

Be My Guest

Traditional and Caribbean Cuisine

Publisher: Charles Knight
Editor/Designer: Dave Geralds
Layout: Beth Formica
Illustrator: William Sonstein
Front Cover Photo: Dennis Anderson Photography
Rear Cover Photos: Jeff Kingstead, Richard Steinmetz
© 1994 Chef Tell Erhardt

Published by: Health Craft, Inc.
5414 Town-n-Country Blvd.
Tampa, FL 33615

Printed in the United States of America
ISBN 1-884784-00-3

Table of Contents

Master Chef, entrepreneur, entertainer, restaurateur - it's hard to find the designation that best describes Chef Tell Erhardt.

Tell was trained in the classic European manner through years of apprenticeships at some of the finest hotels and restaurants in France, Germany and Sweden. Chef Tell gained his first major award at the age of 27, when he received a Gold Medal at the Cooking Olympics and was named "Chef of the Year". In 1970, he also received his Master's Degree in cooking from the University of Heidelberg. He then progressed through the ranks of some of the finest eating establishments in Europe. One of his most ambitious moves was to leave the environment in which he had already achieved recognition and start over in the United States. He did this at the age of 28. Since then, he has achieved national recognition through his appearances on "Evening/PM Magazine", "Hour Magazine," the internationally syndicated "Lifestyles of the Rich and Famous", "Live with Regis and Kathie Lee" and the TNN Network Station.

Despite a hectic schedule, his infinite vitality and enthusiasm remains unabated. He has been appointed Bailli of the Grand Cayman Chapter of the Chaine des Rotisseurs, a gastronomic society founded in 1246. Chef Tell's personality and professionalism has gained many affiliations with his name. From a video tape depicting life and cuisine from the Caymans that is distributed nationally, to infomercials promoting his own line of Chef Tell Cutlery and Stainless Steel Cookware from Health Craft; This German born and internationally trained chef has found continued success in his new home.

To try Chef Tell's cuisine for yourself you need only to travel to Chef Tell's Grand Old House in the beautiful Grand Cayman Islands; or the Harrow Inne in Ottsville, Pennsylvania where Chef Tell purchased and restored this 1744 landmark stagecoach into a signature restaurant. Both restaurants have been acclaimed by press and patrons alike for providing an atmosphere conducive to their surroundings, and at the same time showcasing Chef Tell's popular cuisine. If you are not fortunate enough to visit one of these fine establishments, we hope you will have the time to prepare some of the recipes Chef Tell has made available through this book of recipes. As Chef Tell would say " these recipes are very easy, very simple, no big deal. I see you!"

Appetizers

Be My Guest

CURRIED BEEF IN PASTRY

HEALTH CRAFT
COOKWARE
RECOMMENDED: 2 qt. bowl
9 inch saute pan

INGREDIENTS: 1½ cups all purpose flour
Salt
10 tablespoons butter or margarine
4 tablespoons ice water
2 tablespoons vegetable oil
1 cup minced onion
1 small clove garlic, peeled & minced
1 egg, beaten
1½ teaspoons curry powder
¾ pound lean ground beef
Freshly ground black pepper
Pinch of sugar
3 tablespoons ketchup
1/2 teaspoon cornstarch
1 tablespoon bread crumbs

SERVES: 6

PREPARATION: Put the flour into a bowl with 1 teaspoon of salt. Cut in
the butter, using a pastry blender or two knives, until
the mixture resembles coarse meal. Add only enough
water to combine the mixture until it leaves the sides
of the bowl and forms a ball. Work quickly and do not
overwork the dough. Cover the bowl and refrigerate
while you prepare the filling. Heat the oil in a frying
pan and add the onion and garlic.   Sauté until soft.
Add the curry powder, ground beef, and salt and
pepper to taste. Cook, stirring, until the beef is
browned. Add the sugar and ketchup and cook 2
minutes longer. Remove from the heat. Mix the
cornstarch with the water and stir into the beef
mixture. Add the bread crumbs and mix well. Chill
completely. Divide the dough in half. Roll out one
portion and cut out twelve 2-inch rounds. Roll out the
second portion and cut out twelve two more 2-inch
rounds.

Chef Tell's
Be My Guest
CURRIED BEEF IN PASTRY (Continued)

**PREPARATION
CONTINUED**: Divide the beef mixture evenly among twelve rounds, piling it in the center of each round. Moisten the edges of each round with water. Press a second round of dough over the filling and seal the edges with your fingers.

COOKING: Preheat the oven to 375 degrees. Put the filled past ries on a buttered baking sheet. Brush each with some beaten egg. Bake for 35 minutes or until brown.

SERVING: Put on a tray with doilies or some lettuce leaves.

FRITTATA

**HEALTH CRAFT
COOKWARE
RECOMMENDED:**   11 inch saute pan

INGREDIENTS:
2 eggs, beaten
1 tomato, sliced
2 slices Bermuda onion
1 clove garlic, sliced
¼ cup chopped scallions
Olive oil
2-4 slices red or green pepper
Pepper to taste
2 slices Monterey Jack cheese, optional

COOKING: Heat olive oil. Add the garlic and onion, sauté. Put the eggs on top. In a nice manner, add the tomato slices, pepper, and cheese (if desired). Sprinkle with pepper to taste. Cook slowly and serve.

SERVING: Serve with Breakfast

GERMAN ONION TART

**HEALTH CRAFT
COOKWARE
RECOMMENDED:**

2 qt. bowl
11 inch saute pan
Jelly roll pan

INGREDIENTS:

2½ to 3 cups plus 2 tablespoons all purpose flour
Salt
1 teaspoon baking powder
½ cup plus 4 tablespoons butter or margarine
2 eggs
1/2 plus 3 tablespoons sour cream
4 slices bacon, diced
1½ pounds onions, peeled and sliced thin
½ teaspoon caraway seeds
Freshly ground black pepper
1 egg yolk

SERVES:

12

PREPARATION:

Put 2½ cups of flour in a bowl with 1 teaspoon of salt
and the baking powder. Cut in ½ cup of butter, using
a pastry blender or two knives, until the mixture resembles coarse meal. Beat 1 egg and 3 tablespoons
sour cream together and work into the dough until it
leaves the sides of the bowl and forms a ball. If more
flour is needed, add the additional ½ cup. Cover the
bowl and refrigerate for ½ hour. Then roll the dough
out and fit it into a buttered jelly roll pan, making sure
the dough comes up the sides of the pan. Set aside.

COOKING:

Melt 4 tablespoons of butter in a large frying pan. Add
the bacon, onions, caraway seeds and salt and pepper to taste. Cover and steam until the onions are
very tender

Sprinkle 2 tablespoons of flour over the onions and
mix in.

Be My Guest

GERMAN ONION TART (Continued)

**COOKING
CONTINUED:** Stir ½ cup sour cream, 1 egg, and the egg yolk together and add to the onions. Cook and stir for 3 to 4
minutes. Correct seasonings, if necessary.

Preheat the oven to 400 degrees. Pour the onion
mixture into the prepared crust and bake for 30 minutes, or until the crust is golden and the onions are
browned on top.

SERVING: Serve hot or at room temperature.

NOTE: If you don't have a jelly roll pan, you can use two 9 inch pie pans.

HAM AND LEEK QUICHE

HEATH CRAFT COOKWARE RECOMMEND: Quiche pan

INGREDIENTS:
1 Basic Quiche Crust
4 leeks, white part only
3 tablespoons butter or margarine
Salt
Freshly ground black pepper
2/3 cup diced boiled ham
3 eggs
1½ cups heavy cream

SERVES: 6

PREPARATION: Prepare the Basic Quiche Crust, roll it out, and fit it into a buttered quiche pan. Prick the crust well with a fork.

Wash the leeks well, cut them into small slices, and drain them thoroughly.

COOKING: Melt the butter in a small frying pan. When it is hot, add the leeks and sauté them for 3 to 4 minutes. Season the leeks with salt and pepper to taste. When the leeks begin to get tender, add the ham and sauté for 2 to 3 minutes longer. Remove from the heat and let cool a little.

Preheat the oven to 400 degrees.

Beat the eggs with the cream until thoroughly blended. Stir in the leek mixture and correct the seasonings, if necessary. Pour the mixture into the prepared crust.

Bake for 25 minutes, or until the crust is done and the filling is set and golden.

SERVING: Serve warm.

MUSHROOM STRUDEL

HEALTH CRAFT COOKWARE RECOMMENDED:
11 inch saute pan
Cookie sheet

INGREDIENTS:
2 tablespoons butter or margarine
1 small onion, peeled and minced
1 pound mushrooms, minced
Salt
Freshly ground black pepper
1 8 oz. pkg. cream cheese, softened
12 sheets filo leaves
¼ cup melted butter or margarine
1 cup toasted bread crumbs

SERVES:
12

PREPARATION:
Melt 2 tablespoons of butter in a frying pan. Add the onion and sauté for 5 minutes. Add the mushrooms and salt and pepper to taste. Cook, stirring occasionally, until the mixture is dry. Let the mixture cool for a few minutes, then stir in the cream cheese.

Spread the filo leaves out, keeping those you are not working with covered with a damp towel.

Place one filo leaf in front of you on a clean towel. Brush it with melted butter and sprinkle with a thin layer of bread crumbs. Repeat three more times to make a total of four layers. Do not butter or bread crumb the top layer. Spread one third of the filling down the length of the filo, 2 inches in from the edge. Fold the 2 inch flap of filo over the stuffing, fold in the sides, and roll up the rest of the dough, using the towel as a leverage to pull the roll tight.

Chef Tell's
Be My Guest
MUSHROOM STRUDEL (Continued)

PREPARATION CONTINUED: Put the completed roll on a buttered baking sheet and brush the top of the roll with melted butter. Repeat the entire process two more times with the remaining filo leaves.

COOKING: Preheat the oven to 400 degrees. Bake the rolls for 25 to 30 minutes, or until brown and crisp. Slice and serve warm.

Note: The rolls can be prepared to the end of Step 3 and kept in the refrigerator for several hours or over night. Just cover the rolls with foil before you refrigerate them.

SERVING: Take them out of the refrigerator 1/2 hour before you plan to bake them and keep them covered until just before you put them in the oven. Spread them with more melted butter before baking.

QUICHE LORRAINE

**HEALTH CRAFT
EQUIPMENT
RECOMMENDED:** Quiche pan

INGREDIENTS: 1 Basic Quiche Crust
¼ pound bacon, diced
¾ cup grated Swiss cheese
4 eggs
1 cup heavy cream
2 tablespoons chopped parsley
Salt
Freshly ground black pepper

SERVES: 6

PREPARATION: Prepare the Basic Quiche Crust, roll it out, and fit it into a buttered quiche pan. Prick the crust well with a fork. Sauté the bacon until crisp. Drain it well. Sprinkle the bacon and cheese evenly over the bottom of the quiche crust and press them down lightly.

Preheat the oven to 400 degrees.

Beat the eggs with the cream until thoroughly blended. Add the parsley and salt and pepper to taste. Pour the mixture over the bacon and cheese.

COOKING: Bake for 25 minutes, or until the crust is done and the filling is set and golden.

SERVING: Serve hot.

SEAFOOD QUICHE

HEALTH CRAFT COOKWARE RECOMMENDED: Quiche pan

INGREDIENTS:
1 Basic Quiche Crust
3 tablespoons butter or margarine
1 cup diced assorted seafood, such as shrimp, lobster, scallops, or sole
Salt
Freshly ground black pepper
¼ cup dry white wine
3 eggs
½ cup heavy cream
2 tablespoons chopped parsley

SERVES: 6

PREPARATION: Preheat the oven to 400 degrees.
Prepare the Basic Quiche Crust, roll it out, and fit it into a buttered and floured quiche pan. Spread a layer of dried beans over the bottom of the crust to hold the pastry in place. Bake for 15 minutes. Remove from the oven but do not turn the oven off. Remove and discard the beans and set the partially cooked crust aside.

COOKING: Melt the butter in a small frying pan. When it is hot, add the seafood and sauté for 2 minutes. Add the wine and cook over medium high heat until the wine has evaporated. Remove from the heat and let the mixture cool. Beat the eggs with the cream until thoroughly blended. Stir in the seafood mixture and parsley and season with salt and pepper to taste. Pour the mixture into the partially baked crust. Bake for 30 minutes, or until the crust is done and the filling is set and golden.

SERVING: Serve warm.

STUFFED CUCUMBERS

**HEALTH CRAFT
COOKWARE
RECOMMENDED:** 2 qt. mixing bowl

INGREDIENTS:
3 large cucumbers
1-8 oz package cream cheese, softened
3 tablespoons finely minced onion
½ teaspoon paprika
Salt
Freshly ground black pepper
1 cup finely chopped parsley
Lettuce leaves

SERVES: 6

PREPARATION: Trim the ends off the cucumbers, and cut the cucumbers into 1½-inch lengths. Peel the skin off one half of each segment. Remove the seeds from the center of the sections about two thirds of the way down, leaving the bottom intact. Turn the cucumber shells upside down to drain.

Whip the cream cheese until it is fluffy. Add the onion, paprika and salt and pepper to taste. Form the mix ture into enough small balls to fill the cucumber shells. Roll the balls in the chopped parsley and put one in each cucumber shell.

SERVING: Line six small serving plates with lettuce leaves and distribute the stuffed cucumbers among them. Serve very cold.

STUFFED HAM ROLLS

**HEALTH CRAFT
COOKWARE
RECOMMENDED:**   Chopping board
2 qt. bowl

INGREDIENTS: 1 tablespoon unflavored gelatin
Juice of 1 lemon
1/4 cup of water
1 cup heavy cream
3 tablespoons drained horseradish
12 slices boiled ham

SERVES: 6

PREPARATION: Soften the gelatin in the lemon juice and water. Heat while stirring, to dissolve the gelatin completely. Cool to lukewarm.

Whip the cream lightly (not until it is stiff, but until it just begins to hold stiff peaks). Stir in the horseradish and lukewarm gelatin mixture.

Lay the ham slices on a flat surface so they are not overlapping. Spread the cream mixture evenly over the slices, smoothing it with a small spatula. Chill until the cream mixture thickens a little.

SERVING: Roll the ham slices up and return them to the refrigerator until the cream sets. Serves two rolls per person.

VEGETABLE TERRINE

HEALTH CRAFT COOKWARE RECOMMENDED:
Food processor
2 qt. sauce pan
11 inch saute pan

INGREDIENTS:
½ pound dried white beans, picked over
4 carrots, trimmed, scraped, and julienned
1 cup frozen peas
½ pound string beans; trimmed
1 box fresh brussel sprouts
6 slices trimmed white bread
5 tablespoons butter or margarine
1 small onion, peeled and minced
2 cloves garlic, peeled and minced
¼ pound mushrooms, chopped
2 eggs
1 egg yolk
2 tablespoons chopped parsley
Salt
Freshly ground black pepper

SERVES: 6

PREPARATION: Soak the white beans overnight in water to cover by 1 inch.

COOKING: Drain the beans, add water to cover and salt to taste. Bring to a boil, cover, lower the heat, and cook until tender. Cook the carrots, peas, string beans, and brussel sprouts separately in boiling salted water. Cook each vegetable until it is just barely tender.

Drain each and refresh under cold running water and drain again. Slice the brussel sprouts in half.

Drain the cooked white beans and put them through a food mill to purée them. Set the puréed mixture aside.

VEGETABLE TERRINE (Continued)

COOKING CONTINUED:

Soak the bread in water to cover until it is soft. Squeeze dry and set aside.

Melt 2 tablespoons of butter in a small frying pan. Add the onion and garlic and sauté until soft. Add the mushrooms and cook until the mixture is dry.

Mix together the white bean purée, mushrooms, bread, eggs, egg yolk, and parsley. Season with salt and pepper to taste. Use the remaining butter to butter a terrine mold. (If possible, use a mold with removable sides).

Alternate layers of the bean mixture and the vegetables decoratively in the mold, beginning and ending with the bean mixture.

Preheat the oven to 350 degrees.

Cover the mold tightly with buttered foil, buttered side down. Bake the terrine for 60 to 75 minutes.

SERVING:

Cool, then chill overnight in the refrigerator. Unmold and serve in slices with cornichons on the side.

Chapter 2

Chef Tell's
Be My Guest

Soups

BAHAMIAN FISH CHOWDER

**HEALTH CRAFT
COOKWARE
RECOMMENDED:** 6 qt. pot

INGREDIENTS: 2 cups of assorted fish (grouper, snapper, shrimp,
sword fish, tuna, or other)
1 cup diced carrots
1 cup diced onion
1 cup diced celery
2 cups fish stock or clam juice
2 bay leaves
1 chopped clove of garlic
Salt, pepper and hot sauce to taste
Dash of Cayenne or chili powder
1 tablespoon oil
1 oz. rum (optional)

COOKING: Heat oil to near-smoking point. Add garlic and sauté
until brown. Add carrots, celery, onion and pepper
and sauté approximately 3 minutes at high heat.
Reduce heat and add fish stock, bay leaves and
spices and cook another 10-15 minutes. Add fish and
rum and cook until fish is done. Avoid over-cooking.

SERVING: Serve at once.

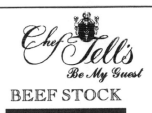

BEEF STOCK

HEALTH CRAFT
COOKWARE
RECOMMENDED: 6 qt. pot

INGREDIENTS:
3 to 4 pounds assorted beef bones and meat, cut up
2 carrots, trimmed and chopped
2 celery stalks, trimmed and chopped
2 onions, peeled and chopped
2 to 3 tomatoes, cored, peeled and chopped
1 bay leaf
3 parsley sprigs
Pinch of dried thyme
Salt to taste
Freshly ground black pepper to taste
12 cups water

YIELDS: 1 1/2 qt.

COOKING:
Put all the ingredients into a large stockpot. Bring to a boil, and simmer, partially covered, for 3 to 4 hours. Skim off any scum that rises to the top.

Strain the stock into a large bowl and discard the solids. Cool the stock, chill it, and remove the fat that rises to the top.

CHICKEN STOCK

**HEALTH CRAFT
COOKWARE
RECOMMENDED:**   4 qt. pot

INGREDIENTS: 2 to 3 pounds meaty chicken bones and giblets, not the liver
1 to 2 carrots, trimmed and chopped
1 to 2 celery stalks, trimmed and chopped
1 onion, peeled and chopped
12 cups water
3 parsley sprigs
1 bay leaf
Pinch of dried thyme
Salt to taste
Freshly ground black pepper to taste

YIELDS: About 1 1/2 qt.

COOKING: Put all the ingredients into a large stockpot. Bring to a boil and simmer, partially covered, for 2 to 3 hours. Skim off any scum that rises to the top.

Guard house

24

Chef Tell's
Be My Guest

CHILLED MANGO SOUP

HEALTH CRAFT COOKWARE RECOMMENDED: Blender

INGREDIENTS:
1 cup mango, peeled
2 cups yogurt
½ cup white wine
Dash of sugar
Mint leaves or slice of mango for garnish

PREPARATION: Combine all ingredients in a blender or food processor. Blend briefly to retain coarse texture; do not puree.

SERVING: Pour into soup plate and garnish with mint leaves or mango slice. Serve immediately. As an option, add a splash of champagne on top just before serving.

Atlantis submarine

COLD FRUIT SOUP

**HEALTH CRAFT
COOKWARE
RECOMMENDED**: 2 qt. mixing bowl

INGREDIENTS: 4 cups water
Piece cinnamon stick
Rind of 1 lemon
1 cup white wine or champagne
3 cups fruit: blueberries, plums, peaches, pears,
apples, etc
½ to 1 cup sugar
Cloves
1 tablespoon cornstarch dissolved in ¼ cup cold water
Garnish: whipped cream

SERVES: 10

COOKING: Bring the four cups of water and the sugar, cloves,
lemon rind and cinnamon stick to a boil. Simmer for
about 30 minutes. Strain. Thicken the soup with the
dissolved cornstarch and cook for a few more minutes.

If using apples, pears, or peaches, peel and dice
them. Skin can be left on plums, if desired.

Add the fruits to the soup and bring to a boil. Remove
from heat and chill.

SERVING: At serving time, stir in the wine or champagne and
serve cold with a dollop of whipped cream for garnish.

COLD ZUCCHINI SOUP

**HEALTH CRAFT
COOKWARE
RECOMMENDED:**   2 2 qt. pots
Blender

INGREDIENTS: 2 pounds zucchini
2 tablespoons butter
2 tablespoons flour
Salt and Pepper
Chopped Parsley
3 cups chicken stock
1 teaspoon marjoram
2 cups milk
1 cup heavy cream

SERVES: 6 to 8

PREPARATION: Wash and slice the zucchini.

COOKING: Cook in the chicken stock until tender. Add the marjoram and puree. Melt the butter and add the flour. Stir and cook for a few minutes and remove from the heat.

Heat the milk. Add the boiling milk to the cooled roux. Stir and cook for about 15 minutes.

Add the pureed zucchini mixture to the white sauce.

SERVING: Season to taste and chill. Mix the cream into the cooled soup. Serve garnished with the chopped parsley.

27

CREAM OF TOMATO SOUP

**HEALTH CRAFT
COOKWARE
RECOMMENDED:** 4 qt. pot

INGREDIENTS:
1 tablespoon olive oil
2 tablespoons butter or margarine
1 large onion, peeled and chopped
4 large tomatoes, cored and cut into eighths, but not peeled or seeded
3 tablespoons tomato paste
Pinch of dried thyme
1 clove garlic, peeled and crushed
¼ cup all purpose flour
3 cups Chicken Stock
2 cups water
Salt
Freshly ground black pepper
Dash of sugar
1 cup heavy cream

SERVES: 6

PREPARATION: Heat the oil and butter together in a deep saucepan. Add the onion and sauté until it is limp. Add the tomatoes and tomato paste and cook for 5 minutes, stirring occasionally. Add the thyme and garlic. Stir in the flour and mix well. Add the stock, water, salt and pepper to taste, and the sugar. Simmer for 30 minutes.

Purée the soup through a food mill or in a blender and then pass it through a sieve to remove any seeds.

COOKING: Return the soup to a clean pan and add the cream. Correct seasonings, if necessary. Heat gently, but do not boil. The soup can also be served chilled.

Be My Guest

CUCUMBER-DILL SOUP

COURSE: Cold soup

HEALTH CRAFT COOKWARE RECOMMENDED: Food processor or blender

INGREDIENTS:
3 cucumbers, peeled and chopped
1 clove garlic, peeled
1 cup plain yogurt
1 cup sour cream
2 tablespoons chopped dill
Salt
Freshly ground black pepper

SERVES: 6

PREPARATION: Put the cucumbers, garlic, yogurt, sour cream, and 1 tablespoon of the dill into the container of a food processor or blender. Purée well and season with salt and pepper to taste. Cover and chill in the refrigerator.

SERVING: Serve the soup in chilled bowls and garnish each serving with a little of the remaining dill.

Kaibo

Chef Tell's
Be My Guest
FISH STOCK

**HEALTH CRAFT
COOKWARE
COOKWARE:**   6 qt. pot

INGREDIENTS: 3 lbs. or more of the bones and heads of non-oily
white-fleshed fish
2 carrots, trimmed and chopped
1 celery stock, trimmed and chopped
1 onion, peeled and chopped
1 bay leaf
3 parsley sprigs
Pinch of dried thyme
Pinch of fennel seeds (optional)
Salt to taste
Fresh ground pepper to taste
1 to 2 cups dry white wine
10 cups of water

YIELDS: About 1 1/2 quarts

COOKING: Put all of the ingredients in a large stock pot. Bring to
a boil and simmer, partially covered for 30-45 minutes.
Remove the scum as it rises to the top.

SERVING: Strain the stock into a large bowl and discard the
solids. Cool the stock, chill it, and remove the fat, if
any, that rises to the top.

NOTE: If you want a more concentrated flavor, return the strained stock to a
clean pan and reduce it, over medium-high heat, until it is half the original
amount.

GAZPACHO

COURSE: Cold soup

**HEALTH CRAFT
COOKWARE
RECOMMENDED:** Blender

INGREDIENTS:

Soup:
1 cup tomato juice
1 small cucumber
1 small onion
¼ cup wine vinegar
1 egg
Juice of ½ lemon
¼ cup half and half
1 whole tomato
1 small green pepper
1 clove garlic
¼ cup olive oil
Salt and pepper
Dash Tabasco

Garnish:
Chopped green pepper
Chopped red pepper
Chopped parsley
Diced tomato
Chopped cucumber

SERVES: 6

PREPARATION: Blend all of soup ingredients in a blender or food processor. Cover and refrigerate. Serve ice cold.

I like to serve this soup from a tureen with plates of chopped vegetables on the side. This way each person can help themselves to whatever garnish vegetables they prefer.

Chef Tell's
Be My Guest

HUNGARIAN GOULASH SOUP

**HEALTH CRAFT
COOKWARE
RECOMMENDED:** 4 qt. pot

INGREDIENTS: 1 pound chuck, flank, or bottom round, diced
3 tablespoons vegetable oil
2 pounds onions, peeled and diced
2 cloves garlic, peeled and minced
1 cup tomato puree
2 tablespoons paprika
1 tablespoon Goulash Spice (see recipe)
2 cups peeled and diced potatoes
1 cup green pepper, seeded and diced
1 cup washed and drained sauerkraut
Water
Salt
Freshly ground black pepper

SERVES: 6

COOKING: Heat the oil in a 4-quart pot. Add the meat and sauté
for 5 minutes, stirring to separate the pieces. Add the
onions and cook until they are golden brown. Add the
garlic, tomato puree, paprika, and Goulash Spice.
Stir well and add water to cover the ingredients by 3
inches.

Bring to a boil and add the potatoes, green pepper,
and sauerkraut. Bring to a boil again, cover, lower the
heat, and simmer for 1½ to 2 hours. Season with salt
and pepper to taste.

SERVING: Serve the soup with bread.

MINESTRONE

**HEALTH CRAFT
COOKWARE
RECOMMENDED:** 4 qt. pot

INGREDIENTS:
Whites of 2 leeks, chopped
2 stalks celery, diced
3 tablespoons butter or oil
2 cloves garlic, crushed
½ cup tomato puree
6 cups beef or chicken stock
2 tablespoons chopped parsley
Salt, Pepper
2 carrots, diced
1 onion, chopped
½ head cabbage, shredded
3 tomatoes, peeled, seeded and diced
1 cup cooked noodles
1 can kidney beans, (optional)
½ cup grated Parmesan cheese

SERVES: 8

COOKING:
Sauté the onion and garlic in oil or butter. Add the
leeks, carrots, celery, cabbage and tomatoes. Season
and sauté for a few minutes. Add the stock and cook
for about 30 minutes or until the vegetables are
tender. Add the kidney beans, if desired, and the
cooked noodles.

SERVING:
When the noodles are hot, add the parsley and
cheese and serve.

ONION SOUP

HEALTH CRAFT
COOKWARE
RECOMMENDED: 4 qt. pot

INGREDIENTS: 2-3 cups sliced onions
3 cups light beef stock (or chicken stock)
2 tablespoons butter
1 clove garlic
1 cup croutons
1 cup grated Parmesan and Gruyere cheese mixed
Salt and Pepper
½ cup white wine (optional)

COOKING: Sauté the onion in butter until golden. Add the white wine, garlic, salt and pepper to taste. Cook for a few minutes to reduce the wine to half. Now add the stock and simmer for additional 20-30 minutes. Pour soup into crocks and top with croutons. Add cheese and top with lots of butter. Bake in oven until cheese is golden brown.

SERVING: Serve this in the Gratin dishes you baked with.

POTATO SOUP

HEALTH CRAFT COOKWARE RECOMMENDED:
6 qt. pot
Blender

INGREDIENTS:
1 pound leeks, sliced
2 pounds potatoes, sliced
6 cups chicken stock
Salt, Pepper, Marjoram
Chopped parsley
½ onion, chopped
3 tablespoons butter or margarine
2 cups cream
4 egg yolks
Bread croutons

COOKING:
Melt butter and sauté onions and leeks until tender. Add chicken stock, salt and pepper, and sliced potatoes. Simmer until potatoes are tender. Purée. Add liaison made by mixing cream with egg yolks. Correct seasonings.

SERVING:
Serve hot garnished with marjoram, chopped parsley, and bread croutons.

SCOTCH BARLEY SOUP

HEALTH CRAFT COOKWARE RECOMMENDED: 4 qt. pot

INGREDIENTS:
¾ pound shoulder lamb with bones
3 quarts water
2 leeks, washed well and julienned
6 trimmed and scraped carrots (2 whole, 4 diced)
6 trimmed celery stalks (2 whole, 4 diced)
2 large onions, peeled (1 whole, 1 diced)
1 bay leaf
3 cloves garlic, peeled and mashed
Salt
Freshly ground black pepper
1 tablespoon vegetable oil
½ cup pearl barley, washed and drained
½ cup heavy cream or half & half
½ cup chopped parsley

SERVES: 6

PREPARATION: Cut most of the meat from the bones and dice it. Set the meat aside in a bowl in the refrigerator. Heat the water, add the bones and any meat scraps, the green part of the leeks, 2 carrots, 2 celery stalks, the whole onion, bay leaf, garlic, and salt and pepper to taste. Bring to a boil, lower the heat, and simmer for 1 hour. Skim off any scum that rises to the top. Strain the stock through a sieve into a large bowl. Discard the solids and set the stock aside.

COOKING: Clean out the stockpot you used to make the lamb stock and add the oil to it. When the oil is hot, add the reserved lamb cubes. Brown them on all sides and add the diced carrots, celery, onion, and white part of leeks. Sauté for 3 to 4 minutes stirring occasionally. Add the barley and strained stock. Bring to a boil, lower the heat, and simmer for 40 to 50 minutes. Remove from the heat and add the cream. Serve each portion sprinkled with parsley.

Chef Tell's
Be My Guest
VEAL STOCK

**HEALTH CRAFT
COOKWARE
RECOMMENDED:** 6 qt. pot

INGREDIENTS:
3 to 4 pounds veal bones and meat, cut up
2 carrots, trimmed and chopped
2 celery stalks, trimmed and chopped
1 to 2 cloves garlic, peeled and chopped
1 bay leaf
3 parsley sprigs
Pinch of dried thyme
Salt to taste
Freshly ground black pepper to taste
12 cups water

YIELDS: 1 1/2 qt.

COOKING: Put all the ingredients in a large stockpot. Bring to a boil and simmer, partially covered, for 3 to 4 hours. Skim off any scum that rises to the top. Strain the stock into a large bowl and discard the solids. Cool the stock, chill it, and remove the fat that rises to the top.

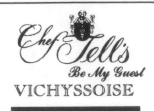

VICHYSSOISE

COURSE: Cold soup

**HEALTH CRAFT
COOKWARE
RECOMMENDED:** 4 qt. pot
Blender

INGREDIENTS: 3 to 4 leeks (white part only) washed well and sliced
1 onion, peeled and diced
4 large potatoes, peeled and sliced
4 cups Chicken Stock
2 whole cloves
1 bay leaf
Salt
Freshly ground black pepper
2 cups half and half
1 cup heavy cream
Chopped parsley or scallions. for garnish

SERVES: 6

COOKING: Combine the leeks, onion, potatoes, and stock in a
sauce pan. Add the cloves, bay leaf, and salt and
pepper to taste. Bring to a boil, cover and lower the
heat. Simmer for 30 minutes, or until the vegetables
are tender.

PREPARATION: Remove the cloves and bay leaf. Cool the
soup and purée it in a blender or food processor.
Refrigerate, covered, overnight.

SERVING: When ready to serve, stir in the half and half and
heavy cream. Correct the seasonings, if necessary.
Serve ice cold, garnished with parsley or scallions.

Chapter 3

Salads

BEET SALAD

HEALTH CRAFT COOKWARE RECOMMENDED:	2 qt. pot 2 qt. bowl
INGREDIENTS:	2 bunches of beets, tops removed ½ onion, peeled and sliced 1 bay leaf ½ teaspoon plus a pinch of caraway seeds cup red wine vinegar cup vegetable oil Pinch of sugar Salt Freshly ground black pepper
SERVES:	6 to 8
PREPARATION:	Do not peel the beets, but wash them well. Put them in a saucepan and add the onion, bay leaf, and ½ teaspoon of caraway seeds.
COOKING:	Add water to cover, bring to a boil, and cook until the beets are tender. Put the beets under cold running water to cool them. Peel and slice them when they are cool enough to handle. Put the sliced beets in a bowl. In a small saucepan, heat the vinegar, oil, pinch of caraway seeds, sugar, and salt and pepper to taste. Pour the hot vinaigrette over the sliced beets. Cover and refrigerate until cool.
SERVING:	Serve in a bowl with fresh chopped onion on top.

CAESAR SALAD

**HEALTHCRAFT
COOKWARE
RECOMMENDED:** 2 qt. mixing bowl

INGREDIENTS: **Dressing:**
2 cups olive oil
8 cloves garlic
Juice of 2 limes (½ cup)
6 anchovies
½ cup grated Parmesan cheese
¼ cup cracked black pepper
Salt to taste
4 egg yolks
1 head of Romaine lettuce, washed and cut into pieces

PREPARATION: Combine the ingredients, except the oil in blender or food processor. Mix thoroughly. Add oil slowly until you reach the consistency of mayonnaise. Mix with washed and cut up pieces of Romaine.

SERVING: Serve on individual plates with croutons and black olives.

CHICKEN SALAD

INGREDIENTS: 2 to 3 cups cooked chicken, diced
2 cans pineapple rings, diced
1 peach, peeled and diced
4 lettuce leaves, shredded
Juice of ½ lemon
¼ cup yogurt
4 tablespoons mayonnaise
Salt to taste
Freshly ground black pepper to taste

PREPARATION: Mix all the ingredients in a bowl.

SERVING: Serve on lettuce leaves garnished with a pineapple slice and a tomato wedge, if desired.

Chef Tell's
Be My Guest
CHICKEN SALAD WITH SPICY PEANUT DRESSING

**HEALTH CRAFT
COOKWARE
RECOMMENDED:**
2 qt. mixing bowl
2 qt. sauce pan

INGREDIENTS:
2 cups cooked chicken, julienned
4 large lettuce leaves
Tomato and lemon slices for garnish
Parsley for garnish
1 cup Peanut sauce

Peanut Sauce:

INGREDIENTS:
1 cup peanut butter
1 cup chicken stock
1 large garlic clove, chopped
2 tablespoons hot sesame oil or spicy oil
6 tablespoons soy sauce
Salt and pepper to taste
¼ cup chopped scallions

COOKING:
Mix first six ingredients of the Peanut Sauce in a large pot. Bring to a boil. Stir until peanut butter is dissolved, let cool. Add scallions, season to taste.

SERVING:
Arrange lettuce leaves on plate, place the chicken in a decorative manner on top. Lace with dressing; garnish and serve.

The wrecks

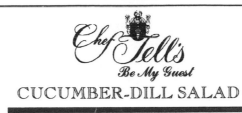

CUCUMBER-DILL SALAD

**HEALTH CRAFT
COOKWARE
RECOMMENDED:** 2 qt. bowl

INGREDIENTS:
4 cucumbers
Salt
1 cup sour cream
2 tablespoons lemon juice
Freshly ground black pepper
Chopped fresh dill
Finely minced onion (optional)

SERVES: 6

PREPARATION: Peel or score the skins of the cucumbers, as you wish. Slice them thin and put the slices in a bowl, salting each layer. Let sit for at least 30 minutes. Drain off the accumulated liquid.

Add the sour cream, lemon juice, and pepper to taste to the cucumbers. Toss well. Add dill to taste and the onion, if desired. Taste for salt and add, if necessary.

SERVING: Serve on a plate covered with lettuce leaves.

ESCOFFIER SALAD

**HEALTH CRAFT
COOKWARE
RECOMMENDED:** 2 qt. mixing bowl

INGREDIENTS: 3 cups cooked roast beef, julienned
1 onion, peeled and sliced thin
½ green pepper, sliced thin
1 small tomato, sliced thin
2 small dill pickles, sliced thin
2 tablespoons ketchup
1 teaspoon Dijon mustard
Dash of Tabasco sauce
Dash of Worcestershire sauce
Salt to taste
Freshly ground black pepper to taste

SERVES: 6

PREPARATION: Combine all ingredients in a bowl. Cover and refrigerate for a few hours to let the flavors develop. If the salad is not tart enough for you, add a little pickle juice.

SERVING: Serve on a nice tray with lettuce leaves and sliced tomatoes.

NOTE: Any cooked meat can be used in this salad.

Chef Tell's
Be My Guest

GERMAN POTATO SALAD

**HEALTH CRAFT
COOKWARE
RECOMMENDED:**   2 qt. bowl

INGREDIENTS: 6 to 8 cooked potatoes, peeled and sliced
½ cup chopped onion
1 to 2 teaspoons chopped parsley
¼ cup red wine vinegar
¼ cup vegetable oil
Pinch of salt
Pinch of black pepper
½ cup warm Chicken Stock

SERVES: 6

PREPARATION: Mix all the ingredients in a bowl, tossing to combine well.

SERVING: Serve in a large bowl and garnish with cucumber slices, pickles or tomato wedges.

a Cayman Classic

Chef Tell's
Be My Guest
GRILLED LOBSTER AND LENTIL SALAD

**HEALTH CRAFT
COOKWARE
RECOMMENDED:**   Hot grill or broiler
2 qt. sauce pan
Mixing bowl

INGREDIENTS: **Marinade:**
½ cup oil
Juice of 1 lemon or lime
Few sprigs of tarragon or a dash of dried tarragon

Salad:
2 cups cooked lentils
½ cup chopped green pepper
½ cup chopped red pepper
½ cup chopped onion
½ cup chopped, blanched carrots
¼ cup red wine vinegar
¼ cup olive oil
Salt, pepper, hot sauce, and nutmeg to taste
2 cloves of garlic, peeled and chopped

PREPARATION: Marinate lobster tails (8-10 oz. each) for 20 minutes.

COOKING: Heat grill and cook tails for approximately 8 minutes. If you prefer, you can substitute shrimp or other fish for the lobster.

Heat oil in a sauce pan. Add garlic, onions, carrots, and peppers. Sauté 2-3 minutes, add the lentils, vinegar and spices.

SERVING: Assemble on a plate with the sliced lobster on top.

NOTE: To cook the lentils bring 6 cups of water to a boil, add 2 bay leaves and 2 cups of lentils, and cook until tender.

HOUSE SALAD WITH GOAT CHEESE

**HEALTH CRAFT
COOKWARE
RECOMMENDED:** Blender
2 qt. mixing bowl

INGREDIENTS: 2 cups Romaine lettuce, cut into bite size pieces
1 cup diced tomatoes
1 cup sliced and peeled cucumbers
½ cup sliced onion
¼ cup chopped scallions
½ cup dressing
½ cup crumbled goat cheese

Dressing:
INGREDIENTS: ½ cup red wine vinegar
½ cup light olive oil, flavored with 6 cloves of garlic (remove garlic before blending)

PREPARATION: Season to taste with a pinch of salt, pepper, tarragon,
oregano, dash of mustard and a few drops of Tabasco
sauce.

Place all ingredients (except garlic cloves) in blender
and blend thoroughly.

Salad:

PREPARATION: Combine all ingredients except cheese in a large bowl.
Toss and let sit for 6-8 minutes. If you use Romaine
lettuce it will remain crisp. Serve with generous portions of crumbled goat cheese.

Be My Guest

PASTA SALAD

HEALTH CRAFT COOKWARE RECOMMENDED: 2 qt. bowl

INGREDIENTS:
1 pound pasta, such as small shells or elbows
½ cup broccoli flowerets
½ cup cauliflower flowerets
1 carrot, trimmed, scraped, and julienned
1 tomato, peeled, seeded, and diced
¼ cup pitted black olives
¼ cup grated Gruyère cheese
2 tablespoons finely chopped fresh basil, or
1 teaspoon dried basil
½ cup red wine vinegar
¼ cup olive oil

SERVES: 6

COOKING:
Cook the pasta in boiling salted water until it is just tender. Drain, then rinse with cold running water, and drain well.

Combine the cooked pasta with all the other ingredients in a large bowl. Toss together to mix completely and let the salad sit for at least 30 minutes so the flavors will blend.

SERVING:
Serve in a large bowl. Garnish with lettuce leaves or tomato wedges

Chef Tell's
Be My Guest
SALAD NICOISE

HEALTH CRAFT COOKWARE RECOMMENDED: 2 qt. mixing bowl

INGREDIENTS:
10 lettuce leaves
1 cup cooked green beans
2 small cucumbers, trimmed and diced
12 radishes, trimmed and sliced
2 - 7 ounce cans tuna fish, drained
1 red onion, peeled and sliced
1 green pepper, seeded and sliced
4 tomatoes, sliced
2 hard cooked eggs, sliced
Anchovies to taste
French dressing

SERVES: 6

PREPARATION: Line a salad bowl with the lettuce leaves. Add the other ingredients, except the dressing, in layers, arranging the tomatoes, eggs, and anchovies decoratively on top.

SERVING: When ready to serve, pour dressing over the salad and toss at the table.

NOTE: Usually people put potatoes in a Salad Nicoise. I don't like them with this mixture, so I don't use them.

The Grand Old House

TOMATO AND CUCUMBER SALAD

**HEALTH CRAFT
COOKWARE
RECOMMENDED:**   2 qt. bowl

INGREDIENTS: 4 cucumbers
Salt
4 tomatoes, cored and cut into wedges
1 cup sour cream
2 tablespoons lemon juice
Freshly ground black pepper
4 tablespoons chopped parsley
4 tablespoons minced onion (optional)

SERVES: 6

PREPARATION: Peel or score the skins of the cucumbers, as you wish.
Slice them thin and layer the slices in a bowl, salting
each layer. Let sit for at least 30 minutes. Drain well.
Add the tomato wedges, sour cream, lemon juice,
pepper to taste, and salt, if needed. Stir in the
chopped parsley and the onion, if desired. Cover and
chill until ready to serve.

SERVING: Serve in a bowl and garnish with parsley sprigs

TUNA AND WHITE BEAN SALAD

**HEALTH CRAFT
COOKWARE
RECOMMENDED:** 2 qt. bowl

INGREDIENTS: 1 cup dried Great Northern beans
½ cup minced red onion
1 7-ounce can tuna fish
Salt
Freshly ground black pepper
1 tablespoon red wine vinegar
2 to 3 tablespoons olive or vegetable oil
Lettuce leaves
1 pint cherry tomatoes, stemmed
Black olives

SERVES: 6

PREPARATION: Pick the beans over and soak them overnight in water to cover by 2 inches.

COOKING: Cook until tender in water without salt. Drain and cool.

In a large salad bowl, mix the beans with the onion. Drain and break up the tuna and add it to the beans. Season the salad with salt and pepper to taste. Mix in the vinegar and oil.

SERVING: Serve the salad mounded on a bed of lettuce leaves, surrounded by cherry tomatoes and black olives for garnish.

YOGURT SALAD - INDIAN RAITHA

**HEALTH CRAFT
COOKWARE
RECOMMENDED:**   2 qt. bowl

INGREDIENTS: 3 cucumbers, peeled, seeded, and diced
3 tomatoes, peeled, seeded, and diced
1 large onion, peeled and diced
Salt to taste
Freshly ground black pepper to taste
Juice of ½ lemon
1 cup plain yogurt

SERVES: 6

PREPARATION: Put all the ingredients in a bowl, toss, and serve.

SERVING: Serve in a bowl garnished with fresh cilander.

Stingray City

FRENCH DRESSING

HEALTH CRAFT COOKWARE RECOMMENDED: Blender

INGREDIENTS:
cup red wine vinegar
cup vegetable oil
cup water
Pinch of sugar
Salt to taste
Freshly ground black pepper to taste

YIELDS: Dressing for 6 salads

PREPARATION: Put all the ingredients into a jar with a close-fitting lid. Shake to combine completely and let stand for 1 hour to develop the flavor.

SERVING: Add to the salad at serving time and toss.

RUSSIAN DRESSING

HEALTH CRAFT COOKWARE: RECOMMENDED 2 qt. bowl

INGREDIENTS:
1 recipe French Dressing
1 hard cooked egg, diced
1 tablespoon minced onion

YIELDS: Dressing for 6 salads

PREPARATION: Combine the ingredients well.

SERVING: Add to the salad at serving time.

MAYONNAISE

**HEALTH CRAFT
COOKWARE
RECOMMENDED:** Food processor or mixing bowl

INGREDIENTS: 1 egg
1 tablespoon red wine vinegar
Pinch of paprika
1 teaspoon Dijon mustard
Salt
Freshly ground black pepper
1½ cups vegetable oil

PREPARATION: Put the egg, vinegar, paprika, mustard, and salt and pepper to taste into the container of a food processor. Blend for a few seconds. With the motor running, add the oil very, very slowly, until the mixture is of the proper consistency. The mayonnaise may be stored in a covered jar in the refrigerator for a week or two.

Pirate's Caves

Chapter 4

Chef Tell's
Be My Guest

Entrees

BEEF ROULADEN

COURSE: Beef Entree

**HEALTH CRAFT
COOKWARE
RECOMMENDED:** 6 qt. pot

INGREDIENTS:
6 tablespoons butter, margarine, or vegetable oil
2 onions, peeled and chopped
6 slices top round
Salt
Freshly ground black pepper
2 tablespoons Dijon mustard
2 tablespoons chopped Kosher dill pickles or
cornichons
1 slice raw bacon, diced
1 carrot, trimmed, scraped and chopped
1 celery stalk, trimmed and chopped
2 cups Beef Stock
1 cup dry red wine
1 tablespoon cornstarch
2 tablespoons cold water

SERVES: 6

PREPARATION: Melt 2 tablespoons of butter in a small frying pan. Add
1 chopped onion and sauté for 5 minutes, or until
golden. Remove from the heat.

Pound the meat lightly and sprinkle the pieces with
salt and pepper. Spread the mustard on one side of
each slice of meat. Distribute the sauteed onion,
pickles, and diced bacon equally among the slices of
meat. Roll the beef slices up and hold closed with
toothpicks.

COOKING: Melt the remaining butter in a frying pan large enough
to hold the rouladen in one layer. When it is hot, add
the beef rolls and sauté them on all sides until they are
browned. Add the remaining onion, the carrot, and the
celery to the pan.

Chef Tell's
Be My Guest

BEEF ROULADEN (Continued)

COOKING CONTINUED:
Stir and brown a little. Add the stock and wine and mix well. Cover the pan and cook over low heat.

Remove the meat to a plate and keep warm. Strain the sauce and discard the vegetables. Return the strained sauce to the pan over low heat. Combine the cornstarch and water to make a thin paste. Slowly add the mixture to the sauce, stirring constantly until the sauce thickens.

SERVING:
Return the meat rolls to the frying pan and coat them with sauce. Serve immediately.

Sea Fan

BRAISED BEEF

COURSE: Beef Entree

HEALTH CRAFT
COOKWARE
RECOMMENDED: 4 qt. pot or dutch oven

INGREDIENTS: 2 tablespoons butter or margarine
1½ to 2 pounds top or bottom round in one piece
1 cup chopped carrot
1 cup chopped celery
1 cup dry red wine
1 cup water
4 tablespoons tomato puree
Salt
Freshly ground black pepper

SERVES: 6

COOKING: Preheat the oven to 375 degrees. Melt the butter in a heavy ovenproof pot. Add the beef and brown on both sides. Remove the beef to a plate and add the vegetables to the pot. Sauté them gently for about 5 minutes. Add the wine, water, and tomato puree to the vegetables and stir in well. Season with salt and pepper to taste. Return the meat to the pot, cover, and bake for 45 minutes to 1 hour.

SERVING: Serve in a bowl or meat plate with some sauce over top.

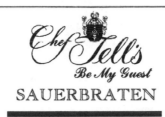

SAUERBRATEN

COURSE:	Beef Entree
HEALTH CRAFT COOKWARE RECOMMENDED:	6 qt. pot
INGREDIENTS:	Salt Freshly ground black pepper 1 4-pound top or bottom round roast beef 2 carrots, trimmed, scraped, and diced 2 celery stalks, trimmed and diced 2 bay leaves 2 cloves garlic, peeled 1½ cups dry red wine 1½ cups dry red wine vinegar 2 cups water 3 tablespoons butter or margarine
SERVES:	6
PREPARATION:	Season the meat with salt and pepper. Combine all the other ingredients except the butter in a glass or ceramic bowl. Add the seasoned meat, cover and refrigerate for 4 to 5 days. Turn the meat twice a day while it is marinating.
COOKING:	When you are ready to cook the meat, melt the butter in an ovenproof pot, remove the meat from the marinade, and brown the meat on all sides in the hot butter. Preheat the oven to 325 degrees. Strain the marinade over the browned beef, cover the pot, and bake for 2½ to 3 hours, or until the meat is tender.
SERVING:	Serve on a tray with some of the sauce poured over. Serve the rest of the sauce in a bowl.

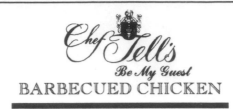

BARBECUED CHICKEN

COURSE:	Chicken Entree
HEALTH CRAFT COOKWARE RECOMMENDED:	Roasting pan 2 qt. sauce pan
INGREDIENTS:	2 chickens Grated peel of 1 orange Grated peel of 1 lemon ¼ cup vegetable oil ¼ cup vinegar ½ cup ketchup ½ cup honey ¼ cup blackstrap molasses ¼ cup chopped onion Juice of 1 orange Juice of 1 lemon Pinch of salt
SERVES:	6 to 8
PREPARATION:	Preheat oven to 375 degrees. Cut the chickens through the back to remove the backbones and breastbones, but leave the chickens attached at the breast area. Flatten the chickens well.
COOKING:	Put them skin side up on a baking sheet and roast for 25 minutes. While the chickens are cooking, make the barbecue sauce by combining the grated orange and lemon peels, vinegar, oil, ketchup, honey, molasses, onion, orange and lemon juices, and the salt in a saucepan. Bring to a boil and cook for 15-20 minutes, or until the sauce is reduced by half. (The color will change from light to dark red as the sauce cooks). When the chickens have cooked for 25 minutes, brush them on all sides with the barbecue sauce. Cook, brushing several times more, until the chickens are tender.

BARBECUED CHICKEN (Continued)

SERVING: Serve with additional sauce if you want.

NOTE: If you like a sweeter sauce, you can add a little brown sugar to the barbecue sauce before you begin to boil it. The chickens can also be cooked on a barbecue grill. Just bake them in the oven for 25 minutes and transfer to the grill, brush with the sauce and cook until done.

CHICKEN BREASTS FLORENTINE

COURSE: Chicken Entree

**HEALTH CRAFT
COOKWARE
RECOMMENDED:**   11 inch pan

INGREDIENTS: 2 10-ounce packages fresh spinach
6 pieces boneless chicken breast
Flour for dredging
¾ cup water
1¼ cups dry white wine
12 tomato wedges
6 lemon wedges
6 anchovy fillets (optional)
Pinch of ground nutmeg
Salt
Freshly ground black pepper

SERVES: 6

PREPARATION: Pick over the spinach to remove the stems and any
bruised leaves. Wash it well and drain it. Blanch the
spinach in boiling water, refresh it under cold running
water, and squeeze it dry. Chop the spinach coarsely.
Pound the chicken breasts lightly to make them even.
Dredge in the flour.

COOKING: Bring the water to a boil in a large frying pan. Put the
chicken breasts into the boiling liquid, cover, and
poach for 5 minutes. While the chicken is poaching,
put the anchovies and the chopped spinach into a
nonstick frying pan. Heat slowly so they do not burn.
Season with the nutmeg and salt and pepper to taste.
Sauté for a few minutes to warm completely.

SERVING: Put equal portions of the spinach on serving plates
and top each with a chicken breast. Pour some of the
poaching liquid over the chicken and spinach and
garnish the dishes with tomato wedges and lemon
wedges. Serve immediately.

CHICKEN POMPADOUR

COURSE: Chicken Entree

**HEALTH CRAFT
COOKWARE
RECOMMENDED:** 11 inch saute pan

INGREDIENTS: 6 pieces boneless chicken breast, skinned
Salt
Freshly ground black pepper
2 eggs
Flour for dredging
2 cups chopped, blanched almonds
6 tablespoons butter or margarine

SERVES: 6

PREPARATION: Pound the chicken breasts lightly to even season them
with the salt and pepper.

Beat the eggs in a flat soup plate. Put a good amount
of flour on wax paper. Put the almonds on a pieces of
wax paper.

Dredge each chicken breast in the flour, dip it into the
eggs and then coat with almonds. Press with the palm
of your hand so that the almonds will stick to the
chicken.

COOKING: Melt the butter in a large frying pan and sauté the
chicken breasts for 4 to 5 minutes on each side, or
until cooked through and golden brown.

SERVING: Serve immediately on a nicely garnished plate.

Be My Guest
COQ AU VIN

COURSE: Chicken Entree

**HEALTH CRAFT
COOKWARE
RECOMMENDED:** 6 qt. pot

INGREDIENTS:
2 chickens, cut into quarters
Salt
Freshly ground black pepper
8 tablespoons butter or margarine
2 onions, peeled and chopped
4 carrots, turned
20 mushroom caps, cut in half
4 tablespoons all purpose flour
2 cups dry white wine
2 cups Chicken Stock

SERVES: 6 to 8

PREPARATION: Sprinkle the chicken with salt and pepper.

Melt the butter in a large frying pan and sauté the chicken until it is lightly browned. Transfer the chicken pieces to an oven proof casserole as they brown.

Preheat the oven to 350 degrees.

COOKING: Add the onions, carrots, and mushrooms to the frying pan and sauté them for 5 minutes. Sprinkle the flour over the vegetables and stir it in. Slowly add the wine, stirring constantly. Stir in the stock and season the sauce with salt and pepper to taste. Bring the sauce just to the boiling point and pour it over the chicken in the casserole. Cover the casserole and bake for 45 minutes to 1 hour, or until the chicken is tender.

SERVING: Serve with noodles with shallot butter.

Be My Guest

CORNISH HENS WITH CABBAGE

COURSE: Chicken Entree

HEALTH CRAFT COOKWARE RECOMMENDED: 11 inch saute pan
Roasting pan

INGREDIENTS:
6 tablespoons butter or margarine
1 large onion, peeled and chopped
2 carrots, trimmed, scraped, and minced
2 apples, peeled, cored, and diced
1 large head green cabbage, cored and shredded
1 cup dry white wine
Juice of 1 lemon
Few juniper berries, crushed
Salt
Freshly ground black pepper
6 small Cornish hens
4 tablespoons vegetable oil
3 tablespoons Cognac
½ cup chopped parsley

SERVES: 6

COOKING:
Melt the butter in a large frying pan and add the onion, carrots, and apples. Sauté for 5 minutes, stirring occasionally. Add the cabbage and cook, stirring, until wilted. Add the white wine, lemon juice, and juniper berries and mix well. Season with salt and pepper to taste. Transfer the mixture to the bottom of a large buttered baking dish.

Preheat the oven to 375 degrees. Sprinkle the hens inside and out with salt and pepper. Brush them with some of the oil. Heat the remaining oil in a frying pan and brown the hens on all sides. As they brown, transfer the hens to the baking dish.

When the hens have all been browned, pour the

CORNISH HENS WITH CABBAGE (Continued)

COOKING CONTINUED: Cognac into the frying pan and stir with a wooden spoon to scrape up any browned on bits in the pan. Pour the sauce over the hens. Roast for 40 minutes, or until nicely brown and cooked. Baste the hens occasionally with the pan juices as they roast.

SERVING: Garnish the dish with the parsley and serve from baking the dish.

NOTE: You may have to use two baking dishes. Just be sure to divide the cabbage mixture and sauce evenly between the two dishes.

ROAST DUCK

COURSE:	Duck Entree
HEALTH CRAFT COOKWARE RECOMMENDED:	Large roasting pan - 2 inches deep
INGREDIENTS:	3 4-pound ducks Salt Freshly ground black pepper Dried rosemary 3 parsley sprigs 3 apples, peeled, cored, and sliced 3 onions, peeled and sliced Water or Chicken Stock
SERVES:	6
PREPARATION:	Preheat the oven to 375 degrees. Sprinkle the ducks inside and out with salt and pepper. Put a pinch of rosemary and a parsley sprig into the cavity of each duck. Put the ducks, breast side down, in a large roasting pan. Put the sliced apples and onions around the ducks in the pan. Pour in enough water to come halfway up the sides of the ducks.
COOKING:	Roast for 1½ hours. Add more water as necessary and stir it into the pan juices. Turn the ducks breast side up and roast for 1 to 1½ hours longer, adding more water, if necessary. Remove the ducks to a serving platter and keep them warm.
SERVING:	Degrease the sauce and strain it. Serve the sauce over the carved ducks.

BAKED STUFFED FISH

COURSE:	Fish Entree
HEALTH CRAFT COOKWARE RECOMMENDED:	9 inch saute pan Roasting pan
INGREDIENTS:	8 tablespoons butter or margarine, softened ½ pound mushrooms, sliced 2 cloves garlic, peeled and minced 1 cup bread crumbs 1 egg Juice of ½ lemon 4 tablespoons chopped parsley Dash of Pernod Salt Freshly ground black pepper 1 3-to 4-pound whole fish such as striped bass, red snapper, or sea trout cleaned & boned 1 cup dry white wine 1 cup Fish Stock, clam juice, or water ½ cup heavy cream
SERVES:	6
COOKING:	Melt 2 tablespoons of butter in a small frying pan and add the mushrooms and garlic. Sauté for 5 minutes, stirring. Remove from the heat and let cool a little. Mix in the bread crumbs, egg, lemon juice, the remaining butter, 2 tablespoons of parsley, the Pernod, and salt and pepper to taste. Preheat the oven to 375 degrees. Sprinkle the inside of the fish with salt and pepper. Stuff with the mushroom filling and close the fish with toothpicks. Put the fish in a baking dish and pour in the wine and stock. Bake for 30 minutes, or until the fish flakes easily.

Be My Guest

BAKED STUFFED FISH (Continued)

SERVING:

Remove the fish from the pan and put it on a serving platter. Remove the toothpicks to make serving easier. Keep the fish warm. To avoid breaking the fish while you are taking it out of the pan, lift it on two long spatulas, one at each end of the fish.

Pour the liquid from the baking pan into a small sauce pan. Bring the sauce to a boil, add the heavy cream, and reduce the sauce a little. Add the remaining parsley, pour the sauce over the fish, and serve hot.

Hibiscus

BLUEFISH PROVENCALE

COURSE: Fish Entree

HEALTH CRAFT
COOKWARE
RECOMMENDED: Roasting pan

INGREDIENTS: 2 to 3 pounds bluefish fillets
Juice of 2 lemons
Salt
Freshly ground black pepper
1 cup bread crumbs
½ cup chopped parsley
½ cup minced onion
4 cloves garlic, peeled and minced
2 teaspoons dry mustard

SERVES: 6

PREPARATION: Preheat the oven to 350 degrees. Put the fillets in a baking dish and sprinkle them with lemon juice and salt and pepper.

Mix the bread crumbs, parsley, onion, garlic and mustard together in a small bowl. Spread over the fillets.

COOKING: Bake for 20 to 30 minutes, or until the fish flakes easily.

Be My Guest

COQUILLES PARISIENNE

COURSE: Fish Entree

**HEALTH CRAFT
COOKWARE
RECOMMEND:**

1 qt. sauce pan
11 inch saute pan

INGREDIENTS:

7 tablespoons butter or margarine
4 tablespoons all-purpose flour
1 cup milk
1 cup Fish stock or bottled clam juice
Salt
Freshly ground black pepper
1 cup grated Gruyère cheese
2 shallots, peeled and minced
¼ pound mushrooms, sliced
1 pound bay scallops
½ cup dry white wine
Juice of ½ lemon
1 chopped truffle (optional)
½ cup grated Parmesan cheese

SERVES: 6

COOKING:

Melt 4 tablespoons of butter in a saucepan and add the flour all at once. Stir until the mixture is smooth and creamy. Cook for 2 minutes, stirring. Remove and let the roux cool.

Heat the milk and the stock together. When it is hot, pour it slowly into the cooled roux, stirring constantly. Season with salt and pepper to taste, bring to a simmer, and cook for 20 minutes. The sauce should be very thick. Add the cheese and stir until it is melted completely. Set the sauce aside.

Melt 2 tablespoons of butter in a frying pan and add

Be My Guest
COQUILLES PARISIENNE (Continued)

COOKING CONTINUED:

Season with salt and pepper and add the scallops, wine, and lemon juice. Cook, stirring occasionally, for 3 minutes, or until the wine is reduced a little. Add the reserved sauce and the truffle and mix well.

Preheat the oven to 400 degrees. Spoon the mixture evenly into 6 scallop shells. Sprinkle the grated cheese over the top and dot with the remaining butter.

Bake for 8 to 10 minutes, or until hot and browned on top. Serve immediately.

Pedro's Castle

Be My Guest

GRAND OLD HOUSE SNAPPER (PAN-FRIED)

COURSE: Fish Entree

**HEALTH CRAFT
COOKWARE
RECOMMENDED:**   11 inch saute pan

INGREDIENTS: 6-8 ounces of snapper or grouper
2 ounces olive oil

Spice Mix:
1 tsp. paprika
1 tsp. sage
1 tsp. marjoram
2 tsp. garlic
6 scallions
1 tsp. hot pepper
1 tsp. black pepper
3 tsp. lime juice
3 tsp. olive oil
Touch of clove

PREPARATION: Combine all herbs and spices. Mix in blender or food
processor and let sit for 2-3 hours, or even overnight.
Put the spice mixture on the fish as desired.

COOKING: Panfry slowly for approximately 8 minutes on each
side.

SERVING: Serve nicely garnished with parsley.

GROUPER WITH COCONUT

COURSE: Fish Entree

HEALTH CRAFT COOKWARE RECOMMENDED: 11 inch saute pan

INGREDIENTS:
6 - 8 ounces of grouper
1 tablespoon butter or oil
Flour for dredging
Salt and pepper to taste
Juice of 1 lemon
¼ cup of fish stock or clam juice
¼ cup white wine
3 tablespoons shredded coconut
2 tablespoons sour cream

PREPARATION: Marinate grouper in lemon juice for 10-15 minutes, then add salt and pepper. Heat oil or butter in sauté pan.

COOKING: Dredge the grouper in flour which keeps fish from sticking to pan. Sauté fish until done on both sides (approximately 8-12 minutes depending on thickness of slices).

Remove fish and keep warm.

Pour lemon juice and wine into sauté pan with all the residue; boil until the volume is reduced by half. Add coconut and sour cream; bring to a boil again. Return fish to pan and re-heat.

SERVING: Place fish on platter, cover with sauce and serve immediately.

SAUTÉED BAY SCALLOPS

COURSE: Fish Entree

**HEALTH CRAFT
COOKWARE
RECOMMEND:** 11 inch saute pan

INGREDIENTS: 6 tablespoons butter or margarine
1½ pounds bay scallops
1½ cups finely chopped carrots
1½ cups finely chopped celery
Salt to taste
¾ cup dry white wine
¼ cup chopped parsley

SERVES: 6

COOKING: Heat a frying pan and, when it is hot, add the butter. When the butter has melted and begun to sizzle, add the scallops and stir. First add the carrots and stir, then the celery and stir. Sprinkle with salt and stir in the wine. Cook for 5 minutes, stirring occasionally.

SERVING: Sprinkle with parsley and serve immediately.

SEAFOOD KABOB

COURSE: Fish Entree

INGREDIENTS: 6 oz. assorted seafood (cut into bite size pieces)
8 pieces of onion (blanched and cut into portions of similar size)
8 pieces of green pepper, (blanched and cut into portions of similar size)

Marinade:
Oil, Ginger, Lime Juice and Tarragon

PREPARATION: Arrange fish and vegetables on a skewer and marinate for 30 minutes or longer. Oil grill lightly to prevent sticking.

COOKING: Grill kabob.

SERVING: Serve on a plate with grilled vegetables.

CAUTION: Don't overcook; you can always return to the grill if needed. After grilling, remove and allow kabob to sit for several minutes to retain juices.

SNAPPER CAYMAN STYLE

COURSE: Fish Entree

EQUIPMENT: 11 inch saute pan

INGREDIENTS: **For 2 servings:**
2 filet of snapper - 4 - 6 ounces
½ cup diced onion
½ cup diced green or red pepper
½ cup tomato concasse, diced (peeled and seeded tomato)
¼ cup fish stock or clam juice
½ teaspoon cornstarch dissolved in water
Salt and pepper to taste
A few drops of Tabasco
1 tablespoon oil
Flour for dredging

PREPARATION: Heat oil in sauté pan. Dredge fish in flour to prevent sticking.

COOKING: Salt and pepper and sauté each side approximately 4-5 minutes. Remove fish and keep warm.

Add remaining ingredients and sauté lightly. Add fish stock or clam juice. Season with Tabasco and cook for 2-3 minutes.

SERVING: Thicken with the cornstarch liquid. When mixture returns to a boil, pour over fish and serve immediately.

Be My Guest
SOLE MEUNIERE

COURSE: Fish Entree

HEALTH CRAFT COOKWARE RECOMMEND: 13 inch saute pan

INGREDIENTS:
6 whole Dover sole, skinned and trimmed
Salt
4 lemons
Flour for dredging
3 tablespoons chopped parsley
4 tablespoons vegetable oil
4 tablespoons butter or margarine, cut in small pieces

SERVES: 6

PREPARATION: Sprinkle the fish with salt and squeeze the juice of 3 of the lemons over the fish. Let sit for a few minutes. Dredge the fish in the flour and shake off any excess flour.

COOKING: Heat the oil in a large frying pan and add the fish. Sauté for 2 to 3 minutes on each side. When the fish is almost cooked, add the butter to the pan and sauté for 3 minutes longer. Remove the fish to a serving platter and keep warm. Cook only two pieces of fish at one time in one pan.

SERVING: Squeeze the juice of the remaining lemon in to the frying pan and add the parsley. Swirl the pan so that everything is combined and pour the sauce over the fish. Serve immediately.

SPICY SHRIMP

COURSE: Fish Entree

**HEALTH CRAFT
COOKWARE
RECOMMENDED:** 13 inch saute pan or a large flambe pan

INGREDIENTS: 36 large shrimp, peeled and deveined, but with tails
left on
3 cloves garlic, peeled and crushed
¼ teaspoon paprika
Juice of 2 lemons
8 tablespoons butter or margarine
1½ cups minced onion
4 tablespoons brandy
1 cup dry white wine
1½ cups peeled, seeded, and diced tomatoes
1½ cups ketchup
Salt
Freshly ground black pepper
1 cup heavy cream
3 tablespoons chopped parsley
1 teaspoons Pernod

SERVES: 6

PREPARATION: Butterfly the shrimp by cutting them almost in half
following the cut already made when you deveined
them. Combine the garlic, paprika, and lemon juice in
a bowl and add the shrimp. Toss the shrimp gently
with two spoons until they are coated with the
mixture. Let them sit for 10 minutes.

COOKING: Melt the butter in a frying pan. When it is hot, add the
shrimp and sauté them, stirring, for 3 minutes. Add
the onion and cook until it is soft. Pour the brandy over
the shrimp and set it aflame. (Be careful not to burn
yourself). When the flames die down, remove the
shrimp from the pan and keep them warm.

SPICY SHRIMP (Continued)

COOKING CONTINUED: Pour the wine into the frying pan and stir it around with a wooden spoon to scrape up all the browned on bits in the pan. Add the tomatoes, ketchup, and salt and pepper to taste. Cook over medium heat until the sauce has thickened. Add the cream and cook down again until the sauce is thick. Sprinkle the sauce with a little more paprika, the chopped parsley, and the Pernod. Return the shrimp to the pan and heat them in the sauce for 1 or 2 minutes.

SERVING: Serve at once over Rice Pilaf.

PORK WITH MUSTARD SAUCE

COURSE: Pork Entree

INGREDIENTS:

6 slices boneless pork loin
Salt
Freshly ground black pepper
Flour for dredging
4 tablespoons vegetable oil
½ cup diced onion
½ cup sliced mushrooms
2 tablespoons Dijon mustard
½ cup dry white wine

SERVES: 6

PREPARATION: Pound the pork slices lightly with a flat mallet.
Sprinkle them with salt and pepper and dredge in flour.

COOKING: Heat the oil in a large frying pan and, when it is hot, add the pork slices. Cook for 2 minutes on each side. Add the onion and mushrooms to the pan and sauté for 3 minutes. Add the mustard and mix well.

Remove the pork slices to a serving plate and keep warm.

Add the wine to the pan and reduce by half.

SERVING: Pour the sauce over the pork slices and serve immediately.

ROAST PORK WITH PRUNES

COURSE: Pork Entree

HEALTH CRAFT COOKWARE RECOMMENDED: Roasting pan

INGREDIENTS:
1 2-to 3-pound boneless loin of pork
Pitted prunes
1 carrot, trimmed, scraped and chopped
1 cup Beef or Chicken Stock
1 celery stalk, trimmed and chopped
1 onion, peeled and chopped

SERVES: 6

PREPARATION: Preheat the oven to 350 degrees. With a sharp knife mark a hole lengthwise through the center of the roast. Enlarge the hole with the handle of a wooden spoon. Push in pitted prunes to fill the hole completely.

COOKING: Put the pork into a roasting pan and roast for ½ hour. Add the vegetables to the pan and roast for 20 to 25 minutes longer, adding a little water from time to time to deglaze the pan.

SERVING: Remove the meat from the pan and let it stand for 10 minutes before carving. Put the roasting pan on top of the stove and pour in the stock. Turn the heat to low, and scrape up any browned-on bits in the roasting pan with a wooden spoon. Pour the sauce over the sliced roast and serve immediately.

Be My Guest

ROAST PORK SHOULDER

COURSE: Pork Entree

**HEALTH CRAFT
COOKWARE
RECOMMENDED:** Roasting pan

INGREDIENTS:
1 5-pound pork shoulder with skin
Salt
Freshly ground black pepper
1 large can of beer
1 large onion, peeled and chopped
1 teaspoon caraway seeds

SERVES: 6

PREPARATION: Preheat the oven to 375 degrees. Score the pork skin diagonally about ½ inch deep. Sprinkle the meat liberally with salt and pepper. Put the meat, skin side down, in a roasting pan. Sprinkle the chopped onion in the bottom of the pan around the meat. Sprinkle the caraway seeds over the onions. Pour about 1/2 inch of hot water into the roasting pan.

COOKING: Roast for 1 hour.

Remove the pork from the pan. Strain the sauce into a bowl and discard the onion bits. Return the pork to the roasting pan, skin side up. Roast for 2 hours, brushing often with the beer. As the roast cooks, deglaze the pan often with the strained sauce.

SERVING: When the roast is finished, remove the skin and cut into pieces. Slice the meat and put two pieces of skin on each serving. Serve the meat with the sauce from the roasting pan.

ROAST TURKEY

COURSE: Turkey Entree

HEALTH CRAFT COOKWARE RECOMMENDED: Turkey Roaster

INGREDIENTS:
1 12-to-18 pound turkey
Salt
Freshly ground black pepper
1 large onion, peeled
4 parsley sprigs
½ cup melted butter or margarine

SERVES: 6 to 10

PREPARATION: Preheat the oven to 375 degrees. Sprinkle the turkey inside and out with salt and pepper. Put the onion and parsley in the cavity of the turkey. Do not bother to truss the bird.

COOKING: Put the turkey on a rack in a roasting pan. Add a little water to the bottom of the pan and roast, uncovered, for 15 minutes a pound. Baste occasionally with the pan juices. When the bird has turned brown, cover it with foil, but baste it every so often.

SERVING: During the last 10 minutes of cooking, baste the turkey several times with the melted butter. Remove the turkey from the oven and let it rest, covered loosely with foil, for 20 minutes. Carve and arrange on a platter. Serve with a Stuffing Loaf or Apple Stuffing (see Vegetables and Starches Section).

VEAL INVOLTINI ALLA MORANDI

COURSE: Veal Entree

**HEALTH CRAFT
COOKWARE
RECOMMENDED:** 11 inch saute pan

INGREDIENTS:
6 veal scallops
Salt
Freshly ground black pepper
6 slices Proscuitto or boiled ham
6 slices Mozzarella or Swiss cheese
6 large fresh basil leaves
4 tablespoons vegetable or olive oil, or a combination of both
1 cup dry red wine
1 cup chicken or veal stock
½ cup tomato puree

SERVES: 6

PREPARATION: Pound the veal scallops lightly with a flat mallet. Sprinkle with salt and pepper. Put a slice of Proscuitto and a slice of cheese on top of each scallop. Top with a basil leaf and roll up and close with a toothpick.

COOKING: Heat the oil in a saucepan large enough to hold the veal rolls in one layer. When hot, add the veal rolls and sauté on all sides for a few minutes. Add the red wine, stock, and tomato puree to the pan and mix well. Bring to a boil, cover, lower the heat, and simmer for 35 minutes, or until the veal is tender.

SERVING: Remove the toothpicks before serving. This is very nice served with pasta.

VEAL - OSSO BUCCO

COURSE: Veal Entree

**HEALTH CRAFT
COOKWARE
RECOMMENDED:** 6 qt. pot
Baking pan

INGREDIENTS: 2 whole veal shanks, cut into 1½ inch thick slices
Salt
Freshly ground black pepper
3 tablespoons vegetable oil
1 onion, peeled and chopped
1 carrot, trimmed, scraped, and chopped
1 leek (white part only), washed well and chopped
2 cloves garlic, peeled and crushed
1 bay leaf
Pinch of dried thyme
1 cup water
2 tomatoes, cored, peeled, seeded, and chopped
3 or 4 tablespoons tomato puree
½ cup dry white wine
2 cups Veal or Chicken Stock (see recipe)

SERVES: 6

PREPARATION: Sprinkle the pieces of veal shank with salt and pepper.

COOKING: Heat the oil in a large frying pan and, when it is hot, add the veal and sauté until brown on all sides. Transfer the veal to a baking pan. Preheat the oven to 375 degrees.

Add the onion, carrot, celery, leek and garlic to the frying pan and sauté for 5 minutes. Add the bay leaf, thyme, and water to the pan and stir with a wooden spoon to incorporate any browned on bits in the pan. Pour the vegetables and sauce over the veal in the baking dish.

Chef Tell's
Be My Guest

VEAL - OSSO BUCCO (Continued)

COOKING CONTINUED: Bake for 1 hour. Add the tomatoes and tomato puree to the veal and mix in well. Bake for 30 minutes longer, or until the veal is tender. Add more water to the pan, if necessary, to keep the meat from sticking.

Add the wine and cook the veal over low heat, stirring with a wooden spoon to pick up any browned on bits in the pan. Add the stock and cook for 15 to 20 minutes longer.

SERVING: Remove the veal shanks to a serving platter. Strain the sauce over the veal and serve with Risotto Parmesan.

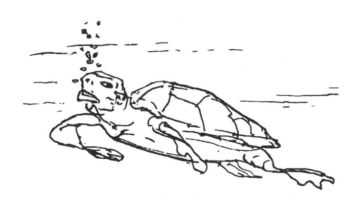

VEAL SCALLOPS WITH MUSHROOMS

COURSE: Veal Entree

HEALTH CRAFT COOKWARE RECOMMENDED: 11 inch saute pan

INGREDIENTS:
1 pound mushrooms, sliced thin
½ cup water
¼ cup dry white wine
Salt
Freshly ground black pepper
6 2-ounce veal scallops
Flour for dredging
2 tablespoons butter or margarine
3 tablespoons chopped parsley

SERVES: 6

PREPARATION: Put the mushrooms, ¼ cup of water, and the wine in a sauce pan. Season with salt and pepper to taste and cook until the mushrooms are tender.

Pound the veal scallops lightly with a flat mallet. Sprinkle with salt and pepper and dredge them lightly in the flour.

COOKING: Melt the butter in a frying pan, add the remaining water   and the veal scallops. Cover the pan and poach the veal until tender, about 15 minutes. Remove the veal to a serving plate and keep warm. Reserve the poaching liquid. Remove the mushrooms from their cooking liquid with a slotted spoon and arrange them around the veal. Reserve the poaching liquid. Pour the mushroom poaching liquid into the veal poaching liquid, bring to a boil and cook until reduced by half.

SERVING: Add the chopped parsley to the sauce, pour over the veal, and serve immediately.

WIENER SCHNITZEL

COURSE: Veal Entree

HEALTH CRAFT COOKWARE RECOMMENDED: 11 inch saute pan

INGREDIENTS:
6 slices boneless veal loin
Salt
Freshly ground black pepper
Flour for dredging
2 eggs, beaten
Bread crumbs for coating
6 tablespoons butter or margarine
6 anchovy fillets
6 thin lemon slices
12 capers

SERVES: 6

PREPARATION: Pound the veal slices with a flat mallet. Sprinkle them with salt and pepper and dredge them in the flour. Dip the veal slices in the beaten eggs and then in the bread crumbs. Press the bread crumbs on with the palm of your hand. Put the breaded veal slices on a flat plate, making sure they do not touch. Separate the layers with wax paper. Refrigerate for 10 minutes before cooking.

COOKING: Melt the butter in a frying pan and add the breaded veal, making sure the veal slices do not touch each other. Sauté for 8 to 10 minutes, turning once, or until the veal is golden brown on both sides.

SERVING: Garnish each piece with an anchovy fillet, a lemon slice, and 2 capers and serve at once.

PAELLA

**HEALTH CRAFT
COOKWARE
RECOMMENDED:** Lasgne pan or skillet

INGREDIENTS:
3 tablespoons oil
1 large onion, peeled and chopped
2 cloves garlic, peeled and minced
1 small chicken, cut up
½ pound boneless pork, diced
½ pound Italian sausage or Chorizo, sliced
Salt
Freshly ground black pepper
2 cups rice
4 cups Chicken stock
Pinch of saffron threads
1 bay leaf
2 tomatoes, peeled, seeded, and diced
12 shelled and deveined shrimp
2 lobster tails, cut into 1½-inch thick slices
12 mussels, cleaned and breaded
12 clams, cleaned and brushed
1 cup frozen peas, thawed and drained
½ cup chopped parsley

SERVES: 6
COOKING: Preheat the oven to 375 degrees. Heat the oil in a
large ovenproof frying pan or paella pan. Add the
onion and garlic and sauté for 5 minutes, stirring
occasionally. Add the chicken, pork, and sausage
and brown them well on all sides. Season with salt
and pepper to taste. Add the rice and stir to coat the
rice with the oil. Add the stock, saffron, and bay leaf.
Bring to a boil on top of the stove and then bake,
covered, for 15 minutes. Add the tomatoes and stir
them in. Distribute the shrimp, lobster, mussels,
and clams decoratively throughout the pan, pushing
them into the rice mixture so they are partially buried.
Sprinkle the peas over the top. Cover again and
bake for 10 minutes. Remove the cover and bake for
5 minutes longer. Remove the cover and bake for 5
minutes longer.

RED CLAM SAUCE

COURSE: Pasta Dish

HEALTH CRAFT COOKWARE RECOMMENDED: 6 qt. pot

INGREDIENTS:
60 littleneck clams in the shells, or 2 cups canned whole clams, drained, with juice reserved
½ cup olive oil
2 cloves garlic, peeled and minced
½ cup chopped parsley
1 tablespoon dried oregano
3 cups tomato sauce

YIELDS: Enough for 1½ pounds pasta

PREPARATION: Clean the clams well, open them, and make sure you catch all the juice.

COOKING: Heat the oil and add the garlic. Sauté for a few minutes, making sure you do not burn the garlic. Add the reserved clam juice, chopped parsley, and oregano and cook for 10 minutes. Add the fresh clams and cook for 5 minutes.

Add the Tomato Sauce and blend well. Cook just to heat through.

SERVING: Serve with linguini but no cheese.

TOMATO SAUCE WITH MEAT
(BOLOGNESE SAUCE)

**HEALTH CRAFT
COOKWARE
RECOMMENDED:** 2 qt. sauce pan

INGREDIENTS: 3 tablespoons Garlic Oil
1 cup chopped onion
1 clove garlic, peeled and minced
1 pound ground round or chuck
1/2 cup Beef, Veal, or Chicken Stock
½ cup tomato purée or tomato paste
1 teaspoon dried oregano
Pinch of ground nutmeg
Salt
Freshly ground black pepper

COOKING: Heat the oil in a large frying pan and add the onion
and garlic. Sauté for 5 to 6 minutes, or until the
onion is soft.   Add the ground meat and sauté until it
loses its red color. Break the meat up with a wooden
spoon as it cooks so that it doesn't lump together.
Add the stock, tomato purée, oregano, and nutmeg.
Stir in well and season with salt and pepper to taste.
Cover and cook over low heat for 20 to 30 minutes.

SERVING: This sauce is very good with little macaroni shells and
grated Romano cheese.

Chapter 5

Vegetables

and

Starches

APPLE STUFFING

**HEALTH CRAFT
COOKWARE
RECOMMEND:** 1 qt. loaf pan

INGREDIENTS:
½ cup butter or margarine
1 small onion, peeled and chopped
4 to 5 tart apples, peeled, cored, and sliced thin
Juice or 1 or 2 lemons
Pinch of sugar
1 teaspoon ground cinnamon
Salt
Freshly ground black pepper
½ pound stale bread or rolls, diced
4 eggs
1½ cups Chicken Stock

PREPARATION: Melt the butter in a large frying pan and add the onion. Sauté for 5 or 6 minutes. Add the apples, lemon juice, sugar, cinnamon, and salt and pepper to taste. Cook for a few minutes, stirring occasionally. Add the bread cubes and mix well.

Mix the eggs and stock together and pour over the bread mixture. Mix well.

COOKING: Pour the stuffing mixture into a large buttered loaf pan and bake along with the turkey for 30 to 40 minutes, or until crisp and golden on top.

NOTE: If you are baking this by itself, set the oven at 375 degrees.

CHEESE POTATOES ANNA

**HEALTH CRAFT
COOKWARE
RECOMMENDED:**   Baking dish

INGREDIENTS: 2 tablespoons butter or margarine
4 large potatoes, peeled and sliced
1 onion, peeled and sliced
Salt
Freshly ground black pepper
½ cup chicken stock
¼ cup grated Parmesan cheese

SERVES: 6

PREPARATION: Preheat the oven to 375 degrees.

Butter a baking dish and layer the potatoes and onions in alternate layers. Sprinkle the layers with salt and pepper. Pour the chicken stock over the vegetables and sprinkle the grated cheese over the top.

COOKING: Bake for 45 minutes to 1 hour, or until the potatoes are tender and the top is browned.

SERVING: Serve in the baking dish with parsley sprinkled on top.

CORN FRITTERS

HEALTH CRAFT COOKWARE RECOMMENDED: 11 inch saute pan

INGREDIENTS:
3 egg yolks
1½ cups cream style corn
½ cup all-purpose flour
Salt
Freshly ground black pepper
4 egg whites
1 cup vegetable oil

SERVES: 6

PREPARATION: Beat the egg yolks until light. Add the corn, flour, and salt and pepper to taste.

Beat the egg whites with a pinch of salt until they are stiff. Fold them into the corn mixture.

COOKING: Heat the oil and, when it is hot, drop the mixture into the hot oil by tablespoons. Cook until brown, turning once. Drain on paper towels

SERVING: Serve hot.

GRATIN OF BROCCOLI

HEALTH CRAFT COOKWARE RECOMMENDED:
4 qt. pot
Gratin pan

INGREDIENTS:
2 large bunches of broccoli, trimmed
2 tablespoons butter or margarine
1 large onion peeled and minced
1 heaping tablespoon all purpose flour
3 cups milk
Salt
Freshly ground bvlack pepper
3 hard cooked eggs, coarsley chopped
1/2 cup bread crumbs

SERVES: 6 - 8

COOKING:
Parboil the broccoli in salted water. Drain well and chop coarsley. Melt 3 tablespoons of butter in a frying pan. Add the onion and saute until soft, about 5 minutes. Add the chopped broccoli and cook and stir until all the liquid has evaporated.

Sprinkle the flour over the broccoli and stir in well. Add the milk a little bit at a time. Stir and wait until the liquid is absorbed before adding more milk. This should take about 15 minutes. Season the broccoli mixture with salt and pepper to taste and stir in the eggs. Preheat the oven to 400 degrees. Coat the inside of the agratin dish with some of the remaining butter. Pour in the broccoli mixture. Sprinkle the top with the bread crumbs and thin slices of butter cut from the remaing butter. Bake for 40 minuts, or until t he top is golden brown. Serve in the baking dish.

NOTE: The casserole may be prepared early in the day and refrigerated until 1/2 hour before you are going to bake it.

PASTA FRESCA

**HEALTH CRAFT
COOKWARE
RECOMMENDED:** Food processor

INGREDIENTS: 2½ cups all-purpose flour
Pinch of salt
5 eggs, lightly beaten
2 teaspoons oil

YIELDS: 1 1/2 lbs.

PREPARATION: Mix the flour with the salt and put it in a mound in the center of a large cutting board. Make a well in the center of the flour and put the eggs and oil into the well.

Begin to mix the dough by adding the flour to the eggs and oil slowly with your fingers until the liquid is all mixed in.

Knead the dough by pushing it away from you with the palms of your hands. First you push the dough away from you, then fold it in half, turn it over, and push again. Do this until the dough is still and shiny. Let the dough rest for about 30 minutes.

Set your pasta machine to the thickest setting. Put the dough through the machine once. Keep resetting the machine and putting the dough through until you get the thickness you want. Flour the dough as you go along so that it doesn't stick to the machine. You will have to cut the dough into smaller portions as the setting on the machine is lowered.

PASTA FRESCA (Continued)

**PREPARATION
CONTINUED:** Cut the pasta into the size you want and let it sit for 5 minutes on a towel or cookie sheet that has been sprinkled with flour. You can also sprinkle the cut noodles slightly with flour so they do not stick together. Cover them with another towel.

COOKING: Cook in rapidly boiling water with two tablespoons of olive oil. These fresh potato noodles cook in 2-3 minutes.

NOTE: The pasta dough can be mixed in a food processor, if you wish. Just put all the ingredients into the container of the processor and blend, turning the machine on and off, until the dough is formed. Let it rest and then proceed to roll the dough through the machine.

Rum Point

PASTA VERDE

**HEALTH CRAFT
COOKWARE
RECOMMENDED:** Food processors

INGREDIENTS: 1 recipe Pasta Fresca
1 10-ounce box frozen chopped spinach, thawed and squeezed dry

PREPARATION Add the spinach to the dough just before you begin to knead it. Incorporate it into the dough as well as you can-it will get more worked in as you knead.

Be My Guest

PASTA VERDE WITH PROSCUITTO

HEALTH CRAFT COOKWARE RECOMMENDED:
Large saute pan
4 qt. pot

INGREDIENTS:
4 tablespoons butter or margarine
1 cup diced proscuitto
½ recipe Pasta Verde or 1½ pounds dried spinach pasta
4 tablespoons chopped parsley
Salt
Freshly ground black pepper
¾ cup heavy cream
4 eggs, lightly beaten
½ cup grated Parmesan cheese

SERVES: 6

COOKING:
Melt the butter in a large pan and add the proscuitto. Sauté for 4 to 5 minutes, stirring occasionally. Remove from the heat and set aside.

Cook the pasta in boiling salted water until it is al dente. Drain and add to the sautéed proscuitto. Add the parsley, salt and pepper to taste, and the cream. Toss well and put over very low heat until it is very hot.

SERVING:
Remove from the heat and add the eggs, tossing to distribute them well. Serve immediately and pass the cheese separately.

PASTA WITH ZUCCHINI

HEALTH CRAFT COOKWARE RECOMMENDED: 13 inch saute pan or flambe pan

INGREDIENTS:
6 zucchini
Salt
6 tablespoons butter or margarine
½ cup finely minced onion
1 clove garlic, peeled and crushed
Freshly ground black pepper
1 teaspoon dried basil, or 1 tablespoon minced fresh basil
1 pound linguini or penne
½ to 1 cup heavy cream
½ cup grated Parmesan or Asiago cheese

SERVES: 6

PREPARATION: Wash and trim the zucchini, but do not peel them. Dice the zucchini, put them in a bowl , and salt them well. Let the zucchini sit for 30 minutes, then rinse and drain them well.

COOKING: Melt 3 tablespoons of butter in a frying pan and sauté the onion for 3 minutes, or until it is soft. Add the garlic, zucchini, salt and pepper to taste, and the basil. Sauté, stirring often, until th zucchini are tender.

Cook the pasta in boiling salted water until it is done al dente.

While the pasta is cooking, heat the remaining butter with the cream in a very large saucepan. Drain the pasta and add it to the saucepan with the cream and the butter. Add the grated cheese and toss well. Add the zucchini and toss again. Serve immediately with extra cheese, if desired, and freshly ground black pepper.

POMMES BOULANGERE

**HEALTH CRAFT
COOKWARE
RECOMMENDED:** 11 inch saute pan
Baking dish

INGREDIENTS: 4 slices bacon, diced
1 onion, peeled and minced
2 tablespoons butter or margarine
4 potatoes, peeled and sliced
Salt
Freshly ground black pepper
½ cup chicken stock

SERVES: 6

COOKING: Sauté the bacon and onion in a small frying pan until the onion is golden and bacon is crisp. Drain off all grease and set aside. Preheat the oven to 375 degrees. Butter the bottom and sides of a baking dish and layer the potatoes in the dish, sprinkling each layer with salt and pepper. Pour the chicken stock over the potatoes. Spread the onion-bacon mixture on top of the potatoes. Bake for 1 hour, or until the potatoes are tender.

SERVING: Serve in the baking dish. Sprinkle with parsley or paprika.

RATATOUILLE

HEALTH CRAFT COOKWARE RECOMMENDED: 4 qt. pot

INGREDIENTS:
4 tablespoons vegetable or olive oil, or a combination of both
1 onion, peeled and sliced
2 pounds eggplant, peeled and sliced
4 zucchini, trimmed and sliced
6 tomatoes, peeled, seeded, and sliced
2 cloves garlic, peeled and minced
Salt
Freshly ground black pepper
¼ cup chopped parsley

SERVES: 6

COOKING: Heat the oil in a large frying pan and add the onion. Sauté for 5 minutes, stirring occasionally. Add the egg plant, zucchini, and tomatoes. Stir in the garlic and salt and pepper to taste. Cover and simmer for 30 minutes, or until all the vegetables are tender and well blended.

SERVING: Sprinkle with parsley to serve. This dish may be served hot or at room temperature. Either way it is good.

RED CABBAGE

**HEALTH CRAFT
COOKWARE
RECOMMENDED:**   2 qt. sauce pan

INGREDIENTS: 2 tablespoons vegetable oil
½ onion, peeled and sliced
1 apple, peeled, cored, and sliced
1 head red cabbage, cored and sliced
1 potato, peeled and diced
1 tablespoon sugar
Pinch of ground cinnamon
Salt
Freshly ground black pepper
½ cup dry red wine
½ cup red wine vinegar
½ cup water
2 tablespoons duck fat or vegetable oil

SERVES: 6

COOKING: Heat the oil in a large saucepan and add the onion and apple and sauté for 5 minutes. Add all the other ingredients and cook, covered, over low heat for 1 hour, stirring occasionally.

SERVING: Correct the seasonings, if necessary. Serve hot.

Chef Tell's
Be My Guest
RICE PILAF

HEALTH CRAFT COOKWARE RECOMMENDED: 1 qt. sauce pan

INGREDIENTS:
3 tablespoons butter or margarine
1 small onion, peeled and minced
1 cup rice
2 cups Chicken Stock, heated
Salt
Freshly ground black pepper

SERVES: 6

PREPARATION: Preheat the oven to 375 degrees.

COOKING: Melt the butter in an ovenproof pot. Add the onion and sauté for 5 minutes, or until it is translucent. Add the rice and cook and stir to coat the rice with the butter. Add the stock, season with salt and pepper to taste, and bring to a boil. Cover and bake for 18 to 20 minutes.

SERVING: Serve with chopped parsley sprinkled over the top.

RISOTTO PARMESAN

**HEALTH CRAFT
COOKWARE
RECOMMENDED:** 2 qt. pot

INGREDIENTS: 4 tablespoons butter or margarine
1 small onion, peeled and minced
1 cup rice
2 cups Chicken Stock, heated
1 bay leaf
Salt
Freshly ground black pepper
1 cup grated Parmesan cheese

SERVES: 6

PREPARATION: Preheat the oven to 375 degrees.

COOKING: Melt the butter in an ovenproof pot. Add the onion
and sauté for 5 minutes, or until it is translucent. Add
the rice and cook and stir to coat the rice with the
butter. Add the stock and bay leaf, season with salt
and pepper to taste, and bring to a boil. Cover and
bake for 18 to 20 minutes.

SERVING: Remove the bay leaf and use a fork to blend in the
grated cheese completely.

STRING BEANS WITH ALMONDS

HEALTH CRAFT COOKWARE RECOMMENDED:
11 inch sauce pan
4 qt. pot

INGREDIENTS:
1 pound string beans, trimmed
½ teaspoons dried winter savory, or lemon juice to taste
Salt
3 tablespoons butter or margarine
Freshly ground black pepper
cup toasted almond slices

SERVES: 6

COOKING:
Cook the beans with the savory in a large pot of boiling salted water until they are just tender, about 5 minutes. The beans should still be quite firm. Drain, refresh under cold running water, and drain again.

Melt the butter in a frying pan and add the string beans. Season with salt and pepper to taste. Cook and toss until hot.

SERVING: Sprinkle with the toasted almonds and serve at once.

STUFFED ACORN SQUASH

HEALTH CRAFT COOKWARE RECOMMENDED:
Baking pan
9 inch saute pan

INGREDIENTS:
4 acorn squash
3 tablespoons butter or margarine
1 small onion, peeled and minced
½ cup sour cream
3 tablespoons brown sugar, or to taste
½ teaspoon ground cinnamon
Salt
Freshly ground black pepper
2 tablespoons chopped parsley
1 to 1½ cups bread crumbs

SERVES: 6

PREPARATION:
Preheat the oven to 375 degrees. Cut the squash in half and scoop out the seeds. Put the squash halves in a baking pan, cut side down, and add ½ inch hot water to the pan.

COOKING:
Bake the squash for 50 minutes, or until the flesh is tender. Cool for a few minutes and scrape out the squash, being careful not to puncture the shells. Purée the squash flesh through a food mill or in a blender or food processor. Put into a bowl and set aside. Melt the butter in a small frying pan and add the onion. Sauté until the onion is golden. Add to the puréed squash with the sour cream, brown sugar, ground cinnamon, salt and pepper to taste, and parsley. Mix well and blend in enough bread crumbs to form a firm mixture. Correct the seasonings, if necessary. Spoon the stuffing into six of the acorn shells and sprinkle some bread crumbs over the stuffing. Bake in a buttered pan for 30 minutes or until piping hot.

SERVING:
Serve right in the baking dish. You may want to garnish with orange slices or parsley.

Be My Guest
STUFFING LOAF

HEALTH CRAFT COOKWARE RECOMMENDED:
Loaf pan
1 qt. pot

INGREDIENTS:
2 loaves stale bread, diced
2 to 3 cups Chicken Stock, heated
6 tablespoons butter or margarine
2 cups diced onion
2 cups diced celery
6 eggs
Pinch of Poultry Seasoning
Pinch of dried thyme
Pinch of dried rosemary
Salt
Freshly ground black pepper

SERVES:
8 to 10

PREPARATION:
Put the diced bread into a large bowl and pour the hot stock over it. Let sit.

COOKING:
Melt the butter in a frying pan and add the onion and celery. Sauté until the onion is golden. Add the onion-celery mixture to the bread with the eggs, poultry seasoning, thyme, and rosemary. Season with salt and pepper to taste and mix well.

SERVING:
Pour the stuffing mixture into a large buttered loaf pan and bake alongside turkey for 1 to 1½ hours. Turn out of the pan and slice to serve.

NOTE: If you are baking this by itself, set the oven at 375 degrees.

Sauces
and
Spices

HERB BUTTER

**HEALTH CRAFT
COOKWARE
RECOMMENDED:**   2 qt. mixing bowl

INGREDIENTS: 1 pound butter
2 tablespoons chopped parsley
Juice of ½ lemon
1 teaspoon salt
½ teaspoon pepper
1-2 cloves garlic, crushed

PREPARATION: Soften the butter well. Mix in the rest of the ingredients.   Roll the butter into parchment paper, forming a
roll with a palette knife. Store in the refrigerator or
freezer. If frozen, cut off a slice at a time, as needed.
Excellent served with grilled meats.

SNAIL BUTTER

PREPARATION: To make snail butter, add a dash of pernod to the herb
butter when mixing it together. Proceed with the
recipe.

PESTO

**HEALTH CRAFT
COOKWARE
RECOMMENDED:**   Food processor

INGREDIENTS: 1 cup fresh basil leaves, washed and dried
6 sprigs parsley
½ cup pine nuts or slivered almonds
2 cloves garlic, peeled and mashed
¼ teaspoons salt
cup grated Parmesan cheese
cup grated Pecorino or Romano cheese
4 tablespoons olive oil
4 tablespoons butter or margarine, softened

SERVES: 10 - 12

PREPARATION: Put all the ingredients into the container of a blender
or food processor and blend until they form a smooth
paste. Put the paste in a jar with a lid and store in the
refrigerator. It will keep about a week.

NOTE: Besides being good on pasta, Pesto can be used to flavor other
dishes, or it can be spread on slices of French or Italian bread and toasted.

CRANBERRY- ORANGE RELISH

**HEALTH CRAFT
COOKWARE
RECOMMENDED**: 2 qt. mixing bowl

INGREDIENTS:
2 oranges
2 cups cranberries
½ cup sugar
1 to 2 tablespoons Kirsch
¼ cup toasted almond slices

YIELDS: 4 - 6 servings

PREPARATION: Peel the oranges completely, making sure you remove all the pith. Cut the oranges into quarters and remove the seeds. Put the oranges and cranberries into the container of a food processor or blender. Grind until they are coarsely chopped. Remove to a bowl and stir in the remaining ingredients. Chill well.

SERVING: Serve with roast turkey or any chicken or roast pork recipe.

ONION AND TOMATO RELISH

INGREDIENTS:
1 cup diced onion
2 cups diced tomatoes
¼ cup chopped parsley
¼ cup red wine vinegar
¼ cup vegetable oil
Salt to taste
Freshly ground black pepper to taste
4 fresh basil leaves, chopped (optional)

PREPARATION: Mix all the ingredients together and let stand for at least ½ hour to develop the flavor.

SERVING: Serve with indian or curry dishes as a condiment.

Be My Guest

FRENCH COCKTAIL SAUCE

**HEALTH CRAFT
COOKWARE
RECOMMENDED:**   2 qt. mixing bowl

INGREDIENTS: 1 cup Mayonnaise
1 tablespoon horseradish
¼ cup ketchup
Juice of ½ lemon
Few drops of Worcestershire sauce
1 to 2 tablespoons brandy
Freshly ground black pepper to taste
½ cup heavy cream, whipped
Salt to taste

PREPARATION: Mix all the ingredients, except the cream, together and
chill. At serving time, fold in the whipped cream and
serve.

SERVING: Serve with chicken fingers, shrimp or crab meat.

REMOULADE SAUCE

HEALTH CRAFT COOKWARE RECOMMENDED: 2 qt. mixing bowl

INGREDIENTS:
1 cup Mayonnaise
2 tablespoons minced pickles
1 tablespoon drained minced capers
2 tablespoons minced onion
1 hard-cooked egg, minced
2 tablespoons minced parsley
Vinegar to taste
2 tablespoons pickle juice
Pinch of dried tarragon
Few drops of Worcestershire sauce
Salt to taste
Freshly ground black pepper to taste

PREPARATION: Mix all the ingredients together, cover, and chill.

SERVING: Serve with fish mousse or any other fish.

RASPBERRY SAUCE

HEALTH CRAFT COOKWARE RECOMMENDED: Blender

INGREDIENTS:
1 cup frozen, thawed raspberries
¼ cup sugar
1 shot Kirschwasser or Fromboise

PREPARATION: Combine in blender or food processor. Mix, strain and serve.

SAUCE ANDALOUSE

**HEALTH CRAFT
COOKWARE
RECOMMENDED:**   2 qt. mixing bowl

INGREDIENTS: 1 cup Mayonnaise
2 tablespoons tomato purée
½ red pepper, peeled and julienned
½ green pepper, peeled and julienned

PREPARATION: Mix all the ingredients together and chill well.

SERVING: Serve with cold chicken or fish.

SAUCE RAVIGOTE

**HEALTH CRAFT
COOKWARE
RECOMMENDED:**   2 qt. mixing bowl

INGREDIENTS: 1 cup Mayonnaise
1 tablespoon cooking liquid from spinach or from
chopped parsley
1 teaspoon chopped fresh tarragon
1 teaspoon chopped parsley
1 teaspoon chopped watercress

PREPARATION: Mix the cooking liquid with the Mayonnaise and fold in
the chopped herbs.

SERVING: Serve with poached eggs or cold fish dishes.

SAUCE TARTARE

**HEALTH CRAFT
COOKWARE
RECOMMENDED:** 2 qt. mixing bowl

INGREDIENTS:
1 cup Mayonnaise
1 tablespoon chopped parsley or chives
1 tablespoon minced onion
1 hard-cooked egg, chopped
1 tablespoon chopped pickles
Salt
Freshly ground black pepper

PREPARATION: Mix the Mayonnaise, parsley, onion, egg, and pickles together. Season with salt and pepper to taste.

TOMATO SAUCE

**HEALTH CRAFT
COOKWARE
RECOMMENDED:**   4 qt. pot

INGREDIENTS: 3 tablespoons vegetable or olive oil
1 onion, peeled and chopped
1 celery stalk, trimmed and chopped
1 small carrot, trimmed, scraped and chopped
1 clove garlic, peeled and crushed
1 large can Italian plum tomatoes chopped
Pinch of dried basil
Pinch of dried oregano
Salt
Freshly ground black pepper

SERVES: 6 -10

COOKING: Heat the oil in a saucepan and add the onion, celery, and carrot. Sauté for about 5 minutes. Add the garlic and tomatoes and mix well. Season with basil, oregano, and salt and pepper to taste. Cook for 30 minutes.

SERVING: Purée the sauce through a food mill. Correct the seasonings, if necessary, and serve hot.

GOULASH SPICE

HEALTH CRAFT COOKWARE RECOMMENDED: Blender or food processor

INGREDIENTS:
Peel of 1 lemon, (yellow part only)
3 cloves garlic, peeled
1 bay leaf
Pinch of dried oregano
1 teaspoon salt
½ teaspoon caraway seeds
Pinch of dried thyme

PREPARATION: Put all the ingredients on a chopping board and mince as finely as possible with a large sharp knife. Store in a tightly closed jar in the refrigerator.

Chapter 7

Desserts

1-2-3 DOUGH

**HEALTH CRAFT
COOKWARE
RECOMMENDED:** 2 qt. mixing bowl

INGREDIENTS:
1 cup sugar
2 cups butter or margarine, softened
3 cups all purpose flour
1 egg

PREPARATION: Combine the ingredients quickly to form a dough. Do not overwork the mixture. Cover and refrigerate for at least 1 hour before using.

NOTE: This recipe can be doubled easily, but it cannot be cut in half. The dough will keep for at least a week in the refrigerator if you cover it tightly.

BLUEBERRY TART

**HEALTH CRAFT
COOKWARE
RECOMMENDED:** Pie pan or quiche pan with removable bottom
2 qt. sauce pan

INGREDIENTS: 1 recipe 1-2-3 dough
2 tablespoons all purpose flour or cornstarch
1 cup lught cream or milk
1 teaspoon vanilla extract
3/4 cup sugar
4 egg yolks
1 cup fresh blueberries
1 tablespoon water
¼ cup apricot jam

PREPARATION: Prepare the dough and line a tart pan with it.

COOKING: Bake blind in a 400 degree oven for 15 minutes or until golden brown. Combine the flour, cream, vanilla, sugar and egg whites in a saucepan. Bring to a boil stirring constantly. Cool quickly by putting the sauce pan into a pan of cracked ice.

Pour the cooked pastry cream into the prepared shell and put the blueberries on top.

Heat the apricot jam with the water and boil the mix ture down a little. Cool slightly and brush the glaze over the blueberries.

SERVING: Chill the tart for 1 to 2 hours before serving.

CHOCOLATE MOUSSE

**HEALTH CRAFT
COOKWARE
RECOMMENDED:**   Double boiler,
2 qt. mixing bowl

INGREDIENTS: 5 ounces sweet chocolate
½ cup heavy cream, whipped
4 egg whites, beaten stiff
Brandy
Kahlua

SERVES: 4

PREPARATION: Melt the chocolate in the top of a double boiler over simmering water. When it is melted, cool it to luke warm. Fold the whipped cream and beaten egg whites into the cooled chocolate and flavor with Brandy and Kahlua to taste.

SERVING: Chill before serving.

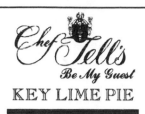

KEY LIME PIE

**HEALTH CRAFT
COOKWARE
RECOMMENDED:**

Pie plate
Mixing bowl
1 qt. sauce pan

INGREDIENTS:

1 cup fresh squeezed lime juice
1 tablespoon Knox plain gelatin
1 - 10 oz. can condensed milk
A few drops of fresh squeezed parsley juice (or green food coloring)
6 beaten egg whites
1 baked pie shell
Grated lime rind (optional)
Whipped cream for garnish

PREPARATION:

Heat gelatin with half the lime juice. In a separate bowl, combine remaining ingredients and mix thoroughly. Add gelatin/lime mixture. Pour into pie shell. Garnish with whipped cream and lime slices. Place in refrigerator or freezer.

SERVING:

Individual slices should be garnished with a lime wedge.

LEMON MOUSSE

HEALTH CRAFT COOKWARE RECOMMENDED
2 qt. sauce pan
2 qt. mixing bowl

INGREDIENTS:
½ cup lemon juice
2 teaspoon grated lemon peel
½ cup sugar
4 egg yolks, beaten
1 cup heavy cream, whipped

COOKING:
Heat the lemon juice, lemon peel, sugar, and egg yolks together in a saucepan. Cook and stir until thickened. Cool and fold in the whipped cream.

SERVING:
Chill before serving.

POIRE BELLE HELENE

HEALTH CRAFT COOKWARE RECOMMENDED:
2 qt. sauce pan

INGREDIENTS:
Pears, 1/2 per person
Chocolate sauce
Sweetened whipped cream
Vanilla ice cream
Toasted almond slices

PREPARATION:
Peel, cut in half and core the pears.

COOKING:
Poach in water with some sugar, lemon juice and a piece of cinnamon stick until the pears are tender. Cool the pears in the liquid until ready to serve.

SERVING:
For each serving, place one pear halve in a dish. On top - place one or two scoops of vanilla ice cream. Pour hot chocolate sauce over the top. Sprinkle with toasted almond slices. Top with sweetened whipped cream.

Be My Guest

WHITE CHOCOLATE MOUSSE WITH RASBERRY SAUCE

**HEALTH CRAFT
COOKWARE
RECOMMENDED:**   1 qt. sauce pan
2 mixing bowls

INGREDIENTS: 1/2 cup sugar
1/2 cup water
4 egg whites, beaten stiff
8 ounces white chocolate, chopped coarse
2 cups heavy cream, whipped

PREPARATION: Bring ½ cup sugar and ½ cup water to a boil and
reduce by half. When egg whites are beaten stiff, pour,
while beating the hot sugar syrup into it. This will cook
the egg whites slightly and they will not weep. Let sit
to cool. Whip the cream and then add the chocolate
into the whipped cream. Fold in the egg whites.

SERVING: Combine and fill in glasses; serve with raspberry
sauce.

NOTE: The mousse will hold in the refrigerator for two days as long as the
raspberry sauce is not put on top.

INDEX

Chef Tell's
Be My Guest

SPECIAL OFFER

Chef Tell Commercial Cutlery
Selected by Chef Tell as the world's finest cutlery
With a lifetime warranty
$119.95
To Order Call:
Health Craft at (813) 885-5244
Or send $119.95 + $7.00 shipping
And applicable sales tax to:
5414 Town-n-Country Blvd.
Tampa, FL 33615
Check, Money Order, Visa, Master Charge and
American Express accepted

Card # _____ Exp. Date _____

Name: _____

Address: _____

Phone: _____

Notes

Notes

Notes

Notes